The Voyage
OF
Archangell

The Voyage

OF

Archangell

James Rosier's Account of the
Waymouth Voyage
OF 1605

A True Relation

Annotated by
David C. Morey

TILBURY HOUSE, PUBLISHERS
GARDINER, MAINE

TILBURY HOUSE, PUBLISHERS
2 Mechanic Street • Gardiner, Maine 04345
800–582–1899 • www.tilburyhouse.com

First hardcover printing: May 2005
10 9 8 7 6 5 4 3 2 1

Library of Congress Cataloging-in-Publication Data
Rosier, James, 1575–1635.
  [True relation of the most prosperous voyage]
  The voyage of Archangell : James Rosier's account of the Waymouth
voyage of 1605, a true relation / annotated by David C. Morey.
       p. cm.
  Includes bibliographical references and index.
  ISBN 0-88448-271-5 (hardcover : alk. paper)
  1. Waymouth, George. 2. Maine—Description and travel. 3. Maine—
History—Colonial period, ca. 1600-1775. 4. Maine—Discovery and
exploration—English—Early works to 1800. 5. America—Discovery and
exploration—English—Early works to 1800. I. Morey, David C., 1942-
II. Title.
  E129.W3R83 2005
  974.1'01—dc22
                              2005002900

The illustration on the jacket front is from an 1897 painting by Jan
Williamson of Cabot's ship *Matthew*.
Jacket and text designed on Crummett Mountain by Edith Allard,
Somerville, ME
Layout by Nina DeGraff, Basil Hill Grapics, Somerville, ME
Copyediting by Barbara Diamond, A Word to the Wise, Litchfield, ME
Production managed by Tilbury House, Publishers, Gardiner, ME
Printing and binding by Maple Vail, Kirkwood, NY
Jackets printed by the John P. Pow Company, South Boston, MA

Look here, my boys; see what a world of ground
Lies westward from the midst of Cancer's line
Unto the rising of this earthly globe;
Whereas the sun, declining from our sight,
Begins the day with our Antipodes!
And shall I die, and this unconquered?
Lo, here, my sons, are all the golden mines,
Inestimable drugs and precious stones,
More worth than Asia and all the world beside;
And from the Antarctic Pole eastward behold
As much more land, which never was descried,
Wherein are rocks of pearl that shine as bright
As all the lamps that beautify the sky!
And shall I die, and this unconquered?
That let your lives command in spite of death.

Christopher Marlowe (1564–93)
Tamburlaine's dying speech to his sons
in Marlowe's play, *Tamburlaine*, c. 1587

[v]

Contents

Preface

THE NARRATIVE OF CAPTAIN GEORGE WAYMOUTH'S 1605 voyage to the Maine Coast is one of the earliest written accounts of the natural resources of northern New England and gives the first description of the Native people who resided here. Most important to Americans though, is that it provided the impetus for the eventual settlement of New England. It was written from the journals of an educated man, sent along on the voyage for the purpose, and, in terms of its prose, is considered the best of the early narratives of English voyages to America. Much of importance has been gleaned from it by historians, ethnologists, and linguists. The chronological accounting of the important activities is nearly complete and gives a good idea of what transpired during the voyage. Rosier's accounting for the latitude positions, distances traveled, winds, and navigation activities are obviously copied from Waymouth's logs. These are too infrequent to be complete, but are useful enough to piece the ocean voyage together. They are altogether absent, however, after the last latitude position taken at Cape Cod on the thirteenth of May. They were either never copied from Waymouth's logs after that date, or they were removed from Rosier's journals in England.

That Captain George Waymouth traveled to the coast of Maine in 1605, in search of a suitable site for a colony to establish a foothold for English sovereignty in America is a fact, not in dispute. He spent twenty-nine days searching, sounding, and exploring a very small area of the coast which included an anchor-age at the Georges Islands and the discovery of a great river. On that river he placed a cross, the sign of discovery and claim, used by all Christian nations of his time. Despite Rosier's clear narrative, there has been uncertainty and controversy about this particular English discovery. Uncertainty because Rosier, by his own admission, did not state, in specific geographic terms, pre-cisely where they had been. The earliest controversy was between the political operatives of the time, over English versus Spanish and French claims and interests, which, in turn, were complicated by Protestant and Catholic religious politics. More recently the controversy has been caused by the uncertainty created by Rosier's, or his editor's, omission of certain key navigational and geographic elements from the narrative, leaving the river which was discovered, in question. That river location and its impor-tance are subjects which are in dispute, and have been since the conclusion of the voyage.

In 1796, while in the course of writing his *American Biogra-phy*, Jeremy Belknap, D.D. needed more information about Captain George Waymouth's voyage, for use in his biography of Waymouth (Belknap, 1794-98). He enlisted the aid of Captain John Foster Williams, of the U.S. Revenue cutter located in Boston, to run along the Maine Coast in an attempt to determine the location of Waymouth's anchorage and river. The opinion of Captain Williams was that Waymouth had anchored at the Georges Islands and discovered the Penobscot River. Belknap wrote Williams's theory into his biography of Waymouth and, until the mid-nineteenth century, the hypothesis was generally accepted.

By the 1850s detractors were reappraising Rosier with a view to crediting the location of the discovery to their own favorite river (Mckeen, 1857) (Sewell, 1859) (Locke, 1859). Some proposed Boothbay and the Sheepscot. Others proposed the Kennebec. But the momentum of the controversy favored the St. George River. Perhaps this was due to the universal acceptance that Waymouth's Pentecost Harbor was at the Georges Islands, six miles south of the mouth of that river.

Two of the proponents of the St. George theory were George Prince of Bath and David Cushman of Newcastle, both of whom were able to convince local historian Cyrus Eaton of Warren in 1858 (Eaton, 1877, p. 15). They promoted their ideas in articles which were published in Volume VI of the Maine Historical Society's Collections (Prince, 1858) (Cushman, 1859). Prince also published his views in the first full-scale editing of Rosier since the 1843 inclusion of it in the Massachusetts Historical Society collections (Prince, 1860). Eaton then published his *History of Thomaston, Rockland, and South Thomaston* in 1865, in which he established publicly, the St. George as Waymouth's river.

After Eaton's *History* of 1865, there was still some grumbling until Alexander Brown of the Virginia Historical Society published his *Genesis of the United States*. In that treatise Brown described the discovery of the Simancas Map (so called) of 1610, in the archive at Simancas, Spain (Brown, 1890, vol. 1, p. 457). It had originally been enclosed in a letter from Alonzo de Velasco, an envoy in London, to Phillip III of Spain and dated 22 March 1611.

At the time it was uncovered, Brown concluded that the Simancus map contained the Saint George River, with a cross clearly illustrated at Thomaston, and most historians, including Maine State Historian, Henry Burrage, agreed. It was considered an extension of evidence on a map by Henry Briggs, purportedly produced in 1616 and published by Samuel Purchas (Purchas, *Pilgrimes*, IV (1625); XIV (1906), p. 424). They proclaimed that it proved conclusively that the river ascended by Waymouth was the St. George River. Presumably, since the St. George River had not been depicted prior to Waymouth, this showed that his map, promised by Rosier in the narrative, but not found or identified since, had contributed, not only to the Briggs Map, but to the Simancas Map as well, at least in this one detail. The cross, too, was described as the cross which Waymouth set where the "river trendeth Westward into the maine."

In 1905 a Tercentenary Celebration of Waymouth's voyage up the St. George River was held, with the raising of a granite cross at Allen Island, costumed reenactments, congratulatory speeches, and a romantic memorial volume (*Waymouth Tercentenary*, 1905). Waymouth's voyage up the St. George has been a closed chapter for most Maine historians—even if not an indelible belief, certainly not worthy of dispute in print.

A hundred years have passed with general acceptance of a theory which cannot be supported by the clear narrative that was used to promote it. This present work is meant to add new information to the debate, as well as to clear up some of the old. The last chapter is taken up with a discussion of the inconsistancies and discrepancies in the Waymouth discovery, as well as the effect we believe that it had on American settlement.

In the publication of this work we leave to our readers the truthfulness of whether the evidence we provide is proof or merely informed speculation. Likewise, we leave the fate of our hypothesis to posterity.

D. C. M.
Tenants Harbor, Maine
May 2005

Apology

TO A MODERN READER, ROSIER'S narrative treatment of the Native American culture which he observed, is filled with the palpable odor of ethnocentrism and raw cultural bias. However jarring this may be to modern Native Americans and enlightened Euro-Americans alike, this is not a characteristic peculiar only to Rosier. The narratives of Christopher Columbus, himself, can inform us of how much Europeans had already improved their behavior by Captain Waymouth's time. As a historian, I cannot apologize for the thoughts, or actions, of the Englishmen who played such enormous roles on the stage which was, arguably, the "discovery" of America—nor should I. My job here is to let these men speak for themselves, and allow their behavior to be judged by the standards which they set for themselves, in their own time. For, those standards, like culture itself, have, necessarily, changed over the four hundred years that have passed.

That said, the nature of this work, treating of two very different cultures, as it does, seems to call out for a statement of the obvious; Those two cultures have not been, and could not be, treated equally here. For that, I apologize.

There is another, albeit more trivial, matter which has presented itself to me in the publication of this work. That is the four hundred-year-old Elizabethan font and vernacular in which Rosier's narrative is written. However quaint I find this form of speech for my own imaginative purposes, I fear it may be a distraction and an obstacle to positive understanding of the places and events described, not to mention downright difficult to read. I have weighed this against my fear that, if modernized, it will become suspect as a product of my own manufacture. My only compromise has been to forego the old English font of the original 1605 edition. If you, dear reader, feel that I have given in to the wrong fear, I apologize.

Acknowledgements

FIRST, I WOULD LIKE TO THANK William Sherwood Cook, a kindred spirit in these matters, who has given me the interest and courage to swim against the tide. Loving thanks to my wife, Amy, whose patience is infinite, for her encouragement and criticism. The help of Earle G. Shettleworth, Jr., Leon Cranmer, Arthur Spiess, and George Carey, all experts concerning Maine's cultures, historic and prehistoric, who have views of their own concerning Maine subjects, in carefully reading mine, was gracious beyond courtesy. Thanks to my publisher, Jennifer Bunting, a stickler for grammatical correctness, who was wonderfully encouraging and helpful to an author with little talent for grammar and prose. Thanks also to Edith Allard whose layout and cover design you see here.

The maps you see here are the work of Rosemary Mosher and Kirsten Read Boettcher, the map ladies of Orbis, Geographic Research and Analysis. As visually delightful as their hand made illustrations are, their knowledge of graphic information systems goes far beyond the use of simple maps to illustrate a narrative.

The Voyage

OF

Archangell

ONE

A Race for the American Coast

V ERY EARLY IN THE SIXTEENTH CENTURY, Spain was jealously protecting her right to the part of the New World which was called Florida, and France had laid claim to Canada or, more specifically, the St. Lawrence. Somewhere between lay a coast whose shores had only cursorily been explored, waiting for any nation having the need, ability, or daring to take it. Based on the North American discoveries of John Cabot in 1497, England could lay claim by original discovery. Being a small, relatively unpopulated nation, and fighting for her own survival, she was not yet suited to the task. By the fourth quarter of the century, however, there were beginning to be Englishmen with enough wealth from fishing and privateering to consider attempts at private adventure. Sir Walter Raleigh and Sir Humphrey Gilbert were prominent among these Elizabethan proponents of the colonization of eastern North America.

Perhaps the greatest single influence on these American ventures was that of Richard Hakluyt who, by 1582, was busy compiling material on all of the English voyages to eastern North America to date, in addition to many of the French. Edward Hayes, Christopher Carleill, and Thomas Harriot were others involved in such promotion.

The English voyages of this period had no particular pattern since the adventurers and promoters themselves each had different interests. Sir Humphrey Gilbert hoped for a colony on Newfoundland, based on the fishing there. Sir Walter Raleigh looked to trade and the gathering of medicinal plants and other wood products. He held, as well, a patent for the colonization of his land of Virginia, issued in 1584 by Queen Elizabeth I, covering a distance of two hundred leagues to the north and south of the Roanoke colony.

Another distinctly different venture in 1582–84 was one whereby Sir Thomas Gerard and Sir George Peckham planned a colony of Catholic landed aristocrats at a location not then known, but based on Verrazano's "Refugio" (now known to be Narragansett Bay). Verrazano's narrative of the 1524 voyage had been published in Italian in 1556 and translated to English in 1582 by Hakluyt, which no doubt had the effect of stirring English interest. This project was advocated, as well, by Sir Humphrey Gilbert, the ever-zealous promoter. Catholic interest was not forthcoming, perhaps by intervention of the Roman Catholic Church or the Spanish who, audaciously, still made claim to the East Coast of North America. Not enough subscribers could be found and the project never got started.

All of the promotion activity in England in the last quarter of the sixteenth century seemed to produce no activity toward the discovery and exploration of what was then vaguely known as Norumbega. Sir Humphrey Gilbert had perished in 1583 on his return voyage from Newfoundland, perhaps dampening the spirits of would-be backers of northern projects. Sir Walter Raleigh's patent and influence had the effect of directing activity to the southward. England's war with Spain, which commenced in 1585, no doubt diverted much of the Crown's financial resources toward military ventures and opened great possibilities for the creation of wealth through privateering in the West Indies, with which promises of earnings from new discoveries could not compete.

By 1600 the lure of Norumbega was just too great to ignore. France had signed the Treaty of Vervins with Spain in 1598, allowing the Jesuit interest in expansion westward and southward in Canada to heat up. Certainly the return of trade goods from New France could not be ignored by wealthy Englishmen looking to increase their fortunes. The East India Company, as well, was beginning to revive the idea of China trade by way of a possible Northwest Passage.

Two projects of note came out of England in 1602. The first was an exploratory voyage sent by the East India Company to find a Northwest Passage. It is only of interest to us here because it is the first glimpse we have of Captain George Waymouth, the explorer. Waymouth, in command, sailed in *Discovery*, of 70 tons, with William Cobreth, master. He had in company *Godspeed*, of 60 tons, with John Drew, master. This was apparently a joint venture between the East India Company and the Muscovy, or Russia, Company and an agent of the Muscovy Company, the Reverend John Cartwright, was along. Waymouth claimed to have had stores enough for thirty-four men to last eighteen months. He made detailed observations of the coast of Labrador and was able to discount Hamilton Inlet as a passage through the continent, but upon arriving at what we now know as Hudson Bay, he was forced by his crew to turn back without actually entering. A serious lack of confidence by other possible backers must have resulted from this performance. Perhaps it was an attempt to restore that confidence that caused him to spend time upon his return writing *The Jewell of Artes*, a treatise on navigation instruments, shipbuilding, guns, and plans for fortified colonial towns, two editions of which he presented to King James I. It seems that his strong interest in exploration and his display of knowledge by that treatise redeemed him, if only temporarily.

Another voyage of 1602 was that of Bartholomew Gosnold. It is of interest here as the first in a series of small ventures from England in the first decade of the seventeenth century, touching on what is now New England. It was through these limited voyages that knowledge and interest were developed which eventually fostered colonization. Little of a specific nature is known of the inception of the Gosnold voyage, or what finally prompted English interest in the land then known as Norumbega. It is certain, though, that the network of wealthy merchant landowners and privateering adventurers was at play. These gentlemen were now looking for new investment opportunities and were, no doubt, receptive to influence by such heavy promoters as Richard Hakluyt and Edward Hayes. The French fur trade just to the north, settlements on Sable Island and at Tadoussac certainly couldn't have gone without notice, and some indication of the promise of excellent fishing might have been available through French, or even English, sources.

In retrospect, we know that the intended destination of the voyage was, once again, Verrazano's "Refugio" of 1524. It also was planned to collect sassafras roots and cedar for return to England, perhaps in imitation of Sir Walter Raleigh's successful projects. Part of the complement was to winter over in America, apparently in an attempt to promote trade with the Native Americans.

The voyage was only partly successful, in that Narragansett Bay was not found. The amount of stores remaining, being only six weeks' supply, was not nearly enough for a six-month winter stay, thereby preventing the winter settlement. On the success side, however, a cargo of sassafras roots and cedar was put aboard.

When Gosnold returned, the organizers quickly found themselves in a legal battle with Sir Walter Raleigh. Although Raleigh had failed to find his lost Roanoke colonists of 1587, he still maintained his title to Virginia. The voyage principals, it seems, had failed to acquire from Raleigh a license for the voyage. At some point a compromise was met and the Brereton official narrative of the voyage contained a dedication to Raleigh and reference in the title to "the discovery of the North part of Virginia." It could be said that this is the point at which the old name, "Norumbega," was officially changed, with the guidance of Sir Walter Raleigh, to the "North part of Virginia." The English, of course, did not recognize the long-used Nova Francia.

The official narrative of Gosnold's voyage was taken from the journals of the Reverend John Brereton, who was probably along as recorder. It was printed by George Bishop in London and bears the unmistakable editorial touch of Richard Hakluyt.

The first edition was so popular that within a few months a completely new and expanded edition was published. It had the distinction of being the first account of a voyage to the still largely undiscovered northern part of Virginia and served nicely as a promotional device for further voyaging out of England to that part of the New World. Another account of the voyage was included in Purchas, *Pilgrimes*, IV, 1625. It was the account of Gabriel Archer, another member of the voyage. Although for some reason not published or made public by Richard Hakluyt, who possessed the manuscript at the time of the voyage, it was passed on to Samuel Purchas before Hakluyt's death. The Archer account, though it does not contain any of the propaganda devices, such as lists of flora and fauna to be found, which we associate with Hakluyt, remains for us a much clearer picture of events as they occurred.

In 1603 another small venture was put together by Richard Hakluyt and several wealthy merchants and inhabitants of the City of Bristol, under the command of Captain Martin Pring. The voyage was made up of the small ship *Speedwell*, of 50 tons, with Pring, Edmund Jones, mate, Robert Salterne, owner's agent, and twenty-seven others. *Speedwell* was accompanied by the bark *Discoverer* with William Browne, master, and thirteen others. In this case the permission of Sir Walter Raleigh was sought and granted, and the voyage began at Bristol on 20 March, a week earlier than the start of Gosnold's voyage a year before.

The commercial plans once again included the gathering of sassafras roots and cedar. No plans were made for a winter settlement, but surveillance for a possible future site for trade was no doubt conducted in and around Cape Cod Bay. There was no attempt to fall back on Verrazano's narrative for direction this time. Perhaps due to the requirements of a diverse group of investors, the profitability of this venture took precedent over exploration for vague promises of wealth from furs, skins, and precious minerals.

For all practical purposes the venture was successful, with a cargo of roots and cedar returned to England in both vessels. The viability of summer exploration of the Cape Cod area was established, even if trade on a commercial level was not yet indicated, and much of the intended trade cargo returned to England. Some hostility had been displayed among the large number of Native Americans there, as well. Harvesting medicinal roots and cabinet-woods seems to have been profitable, although there is some question as to what level of supply the English market would stand.

The similarity of the Pring venture to the Gosnold voyage of 1602 is notable. The starting season was the same within a week. An attempt to find landfall at around 43 degrees north latitude based on Gosnold's charts and instructions is obvious. The choice of Cape Cod as a staging area for their activities was definitely based on information about climate, soil, and availability of sassafras and cedar in the vicinity. The presence of the Bristol merchant, Robert Salterne, who had been on the Gosnold voyage, listed in the later Pring narrative as chief agent, and to whom the narrative was later attributed by Captain John Smith, cannot be ignored. In fact, in regard to these similarities, it is probably safe to say that the Pring voyage was a logical extension or continuation of the Gosnold venture.

In retrospect, the evidence from the Gosnold and Pring voyages, as circumstantial as it is, indicates the heavy influence of Richard Hakluyt as a factor in the organization and planning of these ventures. Here also, a pattern emerges which would indicate that Hakluyt was in a position of some control, though perhaps not financial, and was attempting to find a location with suitable climate, soil, and safety that could induce settlement and act as a portal to the New World. This was being accomplished in a very conservative, even tentative way, so as not to scare off the investors with risky and unprofitable exploratory diversions. A further indication of this control is that even as small as these ventures were, there seems to have been one or more persons along as agent, journalist, or recorder. It could, perhaps, even be said that these recorders were selected by Hakluyt for their ability to gather the information he needed for further promotion or inclusion in his planned new edition of *Principal Navigations*.

Having seen the direction that these early seventeenth-century voyages were beginning to take, we can, perhaps, put the voyage of George Waymouth in 1605 in its proper context as a part of that continuing pattern.

At the abrupt end of the English war with Spain in August of 1604, virtually all of the English military and merchant upper class were faced with reduced fortunes. As in any war the government had run out of money while a wealthy merchant class had found profitable opportunities everywhere. With the ending of hostilities, the future of privateering in the West Indies was uncertain for those who had made their fortunes there. There were a large number of English Catholic soldiers in the Spanish employ who had been exiled during Elizabeth's Protestant reign, who were about to be sent back to England with their loyalty there in question and with little prospect of plying their soldiering trade. Ordinarily this would not seem to be the time for adventuring. It appears, however, that by the time England and Spain were writing the Treaty of London, Richard Hakluyt had stirred a great deal of interest in the discovery and settlement of the northern part of Virginia in America, and exploration in that direction was promoted as a solution to some of these weighty problems.

At least one of the backers proposing the next voyage was Sir Thomas Arundel, a Catholic professional soldier who had distinguished himself in the service of Spain against the Turks, and had been made a count of the Holy Roman Empire. He and another veteran Catholic soldier, Tristram Winslade, commenced plans for an exploratory voyage to find a suitable place to start the transplanting of English Catholics to America, thus reviving an idea that had been put forth in 1582 by Sir Humphrey Gilbert, Sir George Peckham, and Sir Thomas Gerard. Despite his Catholicism, he was the brother-in-law of Henry Wriothesley, the Earl of Southhampton, obviously sincere, and highly respected by James I, who later made him Lord Arundel of Warder. He apparently went ahead with getting the Crown's permission and making plans for the exploratory voyage, while Winslade sought the sanction of Rome and the Spanish monarchy for an eventual colony. Winslade's activities appear to have been more in deference to the Spanish claim to America than the English. Even so, he was in the end, understandably rebuffed.

Regardless of Arundel's favor with James I, apparently his activities and ties to the Spanish government did not receive strong favor amongst other promoters of the voyage, such as the Puritan Lord Chief Justice of England Sir John Popham and his relatives and associates. However naive Arundel's involvement seems in retrospect, he somehow managed to pull the voyage together and get it underway, even if only as a front man for others.

The exploratory voyage of 1605 commenced at Ratcliffe on 5 March without a full complement and proceeded to Dartmouth Haven where the stores and crew were rounded out by the end of March. The ship *Archangell* sailed with Captain George Waymouth, Thomas Cam, his chief mate, and twenty-seven others, including James Rosier, along as voyage recorder, on the first of April 1605. The course was set for the Azores and an attempt was made to hold that direction beyond, to the southwest. Captain Waymouth no doubt did this, as had Gosnold and Pring before him, in order to be able to head into the wind on one tack and make the East Coast of North America, accounting for set to the northward, to make some landfall identified on his charts of the two previous voyages. If he were bound for Buzzards Bay, as is likely, the landfall at Nantucket Shoals was only a few miles too far to the north, but might as well have been a thousand, for his inability to beat southward against wind and current.

After a harrowing and potentially disastrous entry into the worst that Nantucket Shoals had to offer, Captain Waymouth sailed northward until he reached Monhegan. There are indications by Rosier in the narrative that the objective of the voyage had been to the southward, which certainly would have fit the pattern of the two previous voyages, and been yet another revival of Verrazano's "Refugio." That Waymouth seemed never to entertain the idea of returning to the southward is an indication that this voyage was bent on the search for a settlement location and testing trade, regardless of the specific location, with no interest in sassafras or cedar requiring him to return to Cape Cod.

During the stay, most of which was spent anchored at the Georges Islands, much of the time was spent replenishing wood and water supplies, putting together the shallop, doing some local island exploration, and interacting with the Native Americans who visited the area. It was an unhurried and seemingly relaxed affair which Waymouth and Rosier must have thought satisfied the requirements of the backers, without more widespread exploration along the coast.

One of the highlights of the voyage was Waymouth's passage—twenty-six miles with *Archangell* and another forty in a Light Horseman—up a great river, which Rosier describes in considerable detail and in glowing terms. Like other travel writers of the time, he expounded on the virtues of the natural resources as if he were writing a real estate brochure—which he certainly was. His description, however, is not just the cynical hyperbole of a man bent on satisfying the backers of the voyage. These are exclamations any of us, seeing a pristine new land for the first time, might make. After all, *Archangell* was on the coast from 28 May until 26 June, by our Gregorian calendar, in what must have been a fine summer.

In their dealings with the local Indians, Rosier and Waymouth failed dismally at trade. This probably was due to the fact that few skins and furs were actually available, but it also must have been due, in part, to their arrogant and underhanded approach to the process. They were repeatedly visited by Natives from a village on the mainland, just north of their anchorage. Several attempts to have Waymouth approach the Basheba were rebuffed, although on one occasion, charged with mutual mistrust, Waymouth did approach the mainland encampment, only to shy away at the presence of what was said to be "two hundred eighty three Saluages, euery one his bowe and arrowes, with their dogges, and wolues which they keepe tame at command, and not any thing to exchange at all."

Before leaving the coast, Waymouth captured five Natives of a village near the present-day peninsula of Pemaquid. They were removed to England where all lived for at least a year. These young men had experiences which must have been terrifying and still seem incredible to us today. What little we know about their stories has been the subject of some peripheral mention in later narratives and, four hundred years later, is still of great interest. Their generation was the first to be seriously affected by the inevitable march of European civilization into America.

Whether this kidnapping was planned from the inception of the voyage or was an impetuous act on the part of Rosier and Waymouth will probably never be known. The act, however despicable we see it through the prism of four hundred years, was actually common during these tentative explorations. Columbus returned from his first voyage with nine "Indians," simply to prove his discovery. In February of 1495, he sent back to Spain four vessels loaded with Natives, making him one of the greatest purveyors of human cargo, ever. It can be said that most kidnapped Natives from the New World—and there were hundreds, if not thousands—were ultimately sold into slavery in a post-medieval Europe that condoned the practice. If mitigation is possible in this case, Waymouth's five captives were housed in two great households in England and, from what we know, were treated well with the full intent of returning them, unharmed and healthy, to their homeland.

The effects of these kidnappings were understandably far reaching, in terms of negative English/Indian relations, and in retrospect, they also had less than anticipated results in terms of compiling useful information. In the narrative Rosier touted the knowledge received in terms of the language of these five young men and the country of their abode. Of the five hundred Native words he claimed to have translated none were included in the published narrative and only eighty-five survived in the manuscript owned by Richard Hakluyt and passed on to Samuel Purchas. A remarkable document titled *The Description of the Countrey of Mawooshen, discouered by the English, in the yeere 1602. 3. 5. 6. 7. 8. and 9.* also, apparently, resulted from these efforts to interrogate the captives. It too, was among the papers of Richard Hakluyt which, before his death, were passed on to Samuel Purchas, and was included in *Pilgrimes*, IV, 1625. The tract attempts to describe the dominion of the Basheba, a king or super sagamore. The English interlocutors and editors had no prior knowledge of the basic geography of the area these Indians attempted to describe. They also had no understanding of the fact that the placenames given were physical descriptions applicable to, perhaps, more than one place, unlike town and city names in England. Although it has been diligently studied, it has yet to be adequately translated.

Ironically, while Waymouth was on the coast of Maine, Samuel de Champlain was nearby. Waymouth sailed from Pentecost Harbor on 16 June, bound for England. It would appear, from Champlain's narrative, at least, that he passed Allen Island on 1 July, bound from the Fox Islands to the Kennebec.

After making a very brief tour up the Penobscot River to near what is now Bangor, and only a few miles from the winter abode of the Basheba, Waymouth took his vessel back to the Georges Islands to top off wood and water, then sailed for England. An abrupt stop was made on the north edge of Georges Bank because of the shoaling water. There they found fish in large numbers and size, returning some to England as further evidence of their success.

By the time the voyage ended at Dartmouth Haven on 18 July 1605, much had changed with the organizers and backers. Apparently the major supporter and grantee, Thomas Arundel, was not as committed as had been supposed or, more likely, had been displaced by a group of anti-Spanish partners having great influence at court. These detractors, apparently fearful of Arundel's purpose, encouraged his advancement in another field. During the voyage he not only was made a lord, but was given charge of an English mercenary regiment of Catholic soldiers in the employ of the Spanish government in the Netherlands, leaving the

American exploration to others. This arrangement was no doubt orchestrated at the English court and might explain some of the circumstances around the inception and charter of the Virginia Company upon the return of *Archangell*. It might also explain why three of the Natives were put in the custody of Sir Ferdinando Gorges and two others in Sir John Popham's household upon the arrival of *Archangell* in England. Sir Francis Popham, Sir John's son, and Sir Ferdinando Gorges were charter members of the Virginia Company.

Upon his return, Waymouth, apparently on his own account, proceeded to enter into an agreement with Sir John Zouche of Codnor, who was to apply for a royal grant for a settlement in America. It was understood that Zouche, as proprietor, would grant certain secondary rights to Waymouth and others. The agreement was dated 30 October 1605, and was attested to by James Rosier. It appears that Rosier's *Relation* was a prelude to this arrangement which was a naive attempt to capitalize on the Waymouth voyage, even without Arundel or the original backers. The project was an obvious break from Arundel's other partners who were making their own plans toward formation of the Virginia Company. In any case, it was not to be fulfilled, as there was a mysterious delay in approval of the grant by the Lord High Admiral until too late in the season for a voyage, and incidentally, well after the charter of the Virginia Company on 10 April 1606.

Captain George Waymouth was not to be heard from again in regard to the exploration and settlement of America. James Rosier apparently submitted the narrative manuscript to his editor, probably Richard Hakluyt, joined with Waymouth in the Zouche plans, and when that project fell through, disappeared from the scene as well. Whether he was involved in the interrogation of the five captive Indians and the subsequent writing of the *Mawooshen* tract is not known, but is doubtful.

The details of who the original backers were, other than Arundel and Wriothesley, and what their actual intent for this venture was, is not certain, but many aspects of the conduct of the affair bear the pattern of Richard Hakluyt's influence. The narrative of the voyage, although no doubt from Rosier's journals, and for the most part his own words, was certainly edited by Hakluyt. Once again, it was printed by George Bishop in London and contains many of the earmarks of Hakluyt's style, such as reduced narrative of navigation details and movements of the ship, and more detail about the Natives, natural resources, and favorable climate. As was usual, it contained a list of plants, animals, birds, and fishes, some of which could not possibly have been seen by Rosier during his limited stay on the Maine Coast.

At the end of this, the third and perhaps most important voyage of exploration from England, another trend becomes obvious: that of the hired captain. The earlier pioneers of exploration to the new world, such as Raleigh, were seamen with little ability or interest in narrating their adventures. They had a great deal of autonomy in terms of organizing and carrying out their explorations. They were supported by royal purses with only vague promises of riches to return. Title to lands discovered were controlled by the discoverer, in whose name the grant of the Crown was made, usually the captain himself. During the Spanish Wars, wealthy private individuals entered into privateering as investors and outright owners, controlled the operation of their vessels from their own seats at home, and expected a good return. The hired captain became commonplace as the manager of someone else's asset. In this series of early seventeenth-century voyages to America the captains were given token credit for their discoveries, but the evidence is clear that planning and control were reserved for the backers, who had agents along to record the events.

Long since the papal bulls of the early sixteenth century had declared all discoveries to lands "south and west" of Spain to be the exclusive, equally divided right of Spain and Portugal, the English Crown, upon its anti-Catholic stance, had adopted the view that nothing prevented Englishmen from inhabiting any part of the New World that was not already occupied by citizens of another European power. It would be easy to judge these things using the standards of today's international law. That concept, however, was in its infancy in Europe in 1605 and any rules which did exist between nations were usually formulated at the termination of pugilistic hostilities, with the winner imposing the rule. With that as background, the Waymouth voyage of 1605 was seen to be very important to the promotion of English activities aimed at a foothold in America, and coincidentally, a deterrent to Spain's power in the New World. Even so, a modest attempt to mollify the Spanish claim had been made by using Arundel, a Catholic in Spanish favor, as its promoter, and front man. This sham lasted only until the voyage was safely underway, as we have stated, and Arundel was set aside before its return.

James Rosier's narrative, along with promotional activity by Richard Hakluyt, who may have edited it, got investors involved in settlement plans at a time when the Crown could ill afford to bear the cost of expansion into the New World, but certainly had the interest. Shortly after Waymouth's return several plans for the settling of English colonies in America were entertained. Waymouth's crosses on the Maine Coast, along with all this promotional activity, had the effect of staking a claim for the English on a continent where the French were already well entrenched on the north side of the Acadian maritime peninsula, and, at that very moment, looking to expand southward, with tentative settlements already attempted at Port Royal and on the St. Croix River.

As a result of the Waymouth voyage of 1605 and its attendant promotional activity, the scheme that won the day was a plan to form royal colonies here, by chartered companies, under license from the Crown. This, of course, culminated in the formation of the Virginia Company, probably conceived by Sir John Popham, one of the principals, supported by merchants and wealthy landowners influential at court. The charter of the company on 10 April 1606, provided for a South Virginia Group and a North Virginia Group, the South Group under the sponsorship of investors from London and the court, the North Group under the sponsorship of investors from Plymouth, Bristol, Exeter, and elsewhere.

Both groups were to be under the oversight of a royal council made up of investors from each of the geographical areas. The original members of the royal council from the North Virginia Group were Sir Francis Popham (knight), Sir Ferdinando Gorges (knight), Thomas James (Bristol merchant), and James Bagge (Plymouth merchant). The North Virginia Group eventually styled itself the Plymouth Company, and several later voyages were planned and carried out, including its first attempt at colonization, the disappointing Popham Colony of 1607–08. Its fortunes rose and fell over many years, but with the tenacity of Sir Ferdinando Gorges and Sir Francis Popham it held together long enough to see the name of North Virginia changed to New England by Captain John Smith, and the eventual settlement of Plymouth.

T W O

James Rosier's Narrative,
Annotated

THE NARRATIVE OF WAYMOUTH'S VOYAGE, aside from Rosier's rough notes which are probably not extant, exists in two seventeenth-century versions: The version that was printed by George Bishop in London, sometime between the end of the voyage in July 1605 and the early months of 1606, is one. That must be considered Rosier's authorized version. The second version is the manuscript that was apparently in the possession of Richard Hakluyt during his lifetime and was passed by him to Samuel Purchas (Purchas, 1625, p. 1659–67) (Purchas, 1905, p. 335–59). That version contains more narrative in some places than is in the 1605 published version, but much less in other places, indicating that it was edited by Hakluyt or Purchas subsequent to Rosier's original publication.

James Rosier's firsthand account of the voyage, as published, has been reproduced in eight editions since the seventeenth century; (Massachusetts Historical Society's *Collections*, viii, 1843, 125) (Prince, 1860), (Burrage, 1887), (Winship, 1905), (Burrage, 1906), (Levermore, 1912), (Quinn, Quinn, and Hillier, 1979), and (Quinn, 1985). With the exception of the Massachusetts Historical Society printing, the editors of those editions have annotated, as we do here, or at least paraphrased the original work, in an effort to clarify details contained in it, to disseminate the contents to a wider public, and to promote their own conclusions.

In those eight editions, some reproduce Rosier, some reproduce Purchas, and one gives us both for comparison (Quinn,

Quinn, and Hillier). There is no evidence to show Rosier's connection with the changes in the Purchas version in any way. Therefore, to avoid ambiguity, and because there is nothing in the published version with which the Purchas version might conflict, Rosier's originally published edition was chosen as the basis for the present annotation.

The annotations of this edition of Rosier's narrative are stated from the point of view that Waymouth discovered the Penobscot River. For that purpose the annotations make the case and should speak for themselves.

It will be noticed by the reader that there is no attempt to interpret any but the most obvious of Rosier's statements concerning the language and habits of the Natives he interacted with or the flora and fauna of the area which he observed. These subjects have been covered in some detail in works by many authors. It will be noticed, however, that the Native term *Mawooshen* has been used to describe those specific people with whom Waymouth and Rosier came into contact. It is a term later given by one of the captives to describe his own country and people. Variously given as Mawooshen, Mayushon, Mawaushon, it is a compound word of the Eastern Algonquian language family and Eastern Abenaki (so-called) dialect, *M8h8ann-8aessann*. Broken down, the first element *M8h8ann* is "to eat something noble." The second, *8aessann*, is the generic determinative for the meat (flesh) of beasts, whether mammal, molusk, fish, or fowl (Aubery, 1715). It therefore describes a population of people who primarily subsist on meat, or as hunters.

A
TRVE RELATION
of the moft profperous voyage
made this prefent yeere 1605,
by Captaine George Waymouth,
in the difcouery of the land
of Virginia:

where he difcouered 60 miles vp

a moft excellent Riuer; to-

gether with a moft

fertile land.

Written by Iames Rosier.

a Gentleman employed

in the voyage

LONDINI
impenfis Geor. Bishop.
1605.

TO THE READER

EING EMPLOYED IN THIS VOYAGE by the right honourable Thomas Arundell Baron of Warder, to take due notice, and make trve report of the discouery therein performed: I became very diligent to obserue (as much as I could) whatsoeuer was materiall or of consequence in the businesse, which I collected into this briefe summe, intending vpon our returne to publish the same. But he soon changed the course of his intendments; and long before our arriuall in England had so farre engaged himselfe with the Archduke, that he was constrained to relinquish this action. But the commodities and profits of the countrey, together with the fitnesse of plantation, being by some honourable gentlemen of good woorth and qualitie, and merchants of good sufficiency and iudgement duly considered, have at their owne charge (intending both their priuate and the common benefit of their countrey) vndertaken the transporting of a Colony for the plantation thereof; being much encouraged thereunto by the gracious fauour of the Kings Maiesty himselfe, and diuers Lords of his Highnesse most honourable Priuie Councell.[1] After these proposed designes were concluded, I was animated to publish this briefe relation, and not before; be-

[1] We must take Rosier (and/or his editor) at his word here. There was tremendous activity at Plymouth and at London during the months following Waymouth's return. The reports from the crew must have been glowing, not to mention the presence of five Abenakis in England, not quite as savage as previously supposed. Surely this statement was based on the activities of the Lord Chief Justice, Sir John Popham, and others, in preparation for the forming of the Virginia Company, which were well underway by the time of publishing. Sir Ferdinando Gorges (commander of the fort at Plymouth, by this time having in custody three of the five Natives captured by Waymouth) certainly was a party to the promotion of a new venture.

cause some forrein Nation (being fully assured of the fruitfulnesse of the countrie) haue hoped hereby to gaine some knowledge of the place, seeing they could not allure our Captaine or any speciall man of our Company to combine with them for their direction, nor obtaine their purpose, in conueying away our Saluages, which was busily in practise. And this is the cause that I haue neither written of the latitude or variation most exactly obserued by our Captaine with sundrie instruments, which together with his perfect Geographicall Map of the countrey, he entendeth hereafter to set forth.[2] I haue likewise purposedly omitted here to adde a collection of many words in their language to the number of foure or fiue hundred, as also the names of diuers of their governours, as well their friends as their enemies; being reserued to be made knowen for the benefit of those that shal goe in the next

---

[2] The fact that Rosier only states Waymouth's intent to publish indicates that at the time of the publishing of his *Relation* there was no map available. His use of the phrase "perfect Geographicall Map of the countrey" seems a bit naive in that the country explored by Waymouth (albeit accurately sounded and observed) was confined to one river. The map alluded to has never been found or cited in any subsequent writings nor has it left any positively identifiable evidence of its existence on any other map.

Much has been said about Spain's attempts to gather information from this voyage for its own purposes. These fears, if Rosier's remark about Waymouth and others being approached by agents of that country are true, were no doubt well founded. We must also remember that the backer, Thomas Arundel, had earlier been made a count of the Holy Roman Empire by the King of Spain, and was probably greatly suspect, himself. If these are the reasons a map was never produced, the new English backers apparently were left in the dark as well. The subsequent activities of the Plymouth Company would indicate that they, too, had no idea precisely where Waymouth had been. In all likelihood, at the time, Waymouth's map was not only not published, but never left Waymouth's possession.

voyage.[3] But our particular proceedings in the whole discouerie, the commodious situation of the riuer, the fertilitie of the land, with the profits there to be had, and here reported, I refer to be verified by the whole Company, as being eye-witnesses of my words, and most of them neere inhabitants vpon the Thames. So with my prayers to God for the conuersion of so ingenious and well disposed people, and for the prosperous successiue euents of the noble intenders the prosecution thereof, I rest.

Your Friend I.R.

[3] It is unfortunate that Rosier did not include his collection of Eastern Abenaki words with his interpretation of their English equivalents. What we do have comes thirdhand (Rosier to Hakluyt to Purchas) and contains no placenames at all. Such a large list as four or five hundred words might shed more light on the patterns of Elizabethan phonetic spelling and pronunciation of Indian words, as well as what Rosier understood while interpreting at Pentecost Harbor.

A TRUE RELATION

of *Captaine George Waymouth* his
Voyage, made this present yeere
1605: *in the Discouery of*
the North part of
Virginia.

PON TUESDAY THE 5 DAY OF MARCH, about ten a clocke afore noone, we set saile from Ratcliffe, and came to an anker that tide about two a clocke before grauesend.

From thence the 10 of March being Sunday at night we ankered in the Downes; and there rode til the next day about three a clocke after noone when with a scant winde we set saile; and by reason the winde continued Southwardly, we were beaten vp and downe: but on Saturday the 16 day about foure a clocke after noon we put into Dartmouth hauen, where the continuance of the winde at South & South-west constrained vs to ride till the last of this moneth.[4] There we shipped some of our men, and supplied necessaries for our ship and voyage.

Vpon Easter day, being the last of March, the winde comming at North-North-East, about fiue a clocke after noon, we wayed anker, and put to sea, In the name of God, being well vict-ualled and furnished with munition and all necessaries: Our whole

---

[4] Dartmouth would likely have been the last stop before setting out, in any case. The time usually encountered to get to that point would eat into the stores and water, causing any prudent seaman to take advantage of the last safe anchorage to top off, as well as to watch the weather. It is somewhat surprising that he waited until that point to ship more crew-men, considering the nature of the voyage. This could also indicate that he was unable to attract enough good seamen in the Thames who were willing to risk such an uncertain voyage.

company being but 29 persons; of whom I may boldly say, few voyages haue beene manned forth with better Sea-men generally in respect of our small number.[5]

Munday the next day, being the first of Aprill, by sixe a clocke in the morning we were sixe leagues South-South-East from the Lizarde.

At two a clocke in the afternoone this day, the weather being very faire, our Captaine for his own experience and others with him sounded, and had sixe and fiftie fathoms and a halfe. The sounding was some small black perrie sand, some reddish sand, a match or two, with small shels called Saint Iames his shels.

The foureteenth of Aprill being Sunday, betweene nine and ten of the clocke in the morning our Captaine descried the Iland of Cueruo:[6] which bare South-West and by West, about seuen leagues from vs: by eleuen of the clocke we descried Flores to the Southward of Cueruo, as it lieth: by foure a clocke in the afternoone we brought Cueruo due South from vs within two leagues

---

[5] This statement could be taken simply as an endorsement of the talents of the crew, but his emphasis on the fact that the whole company was "but 29 persons" and that they were good, considering the small number, seems to further reinforce the implication that she may have sailed short of crew.

[6] The winds remained favorable for several days. *Archangell* covered some 1,200 nautical miles, making her average speed 3.6 knots, even though she would have been bucking the prevailing currents along her trackline, which are always from the west and south due to that part of the Gulf Stream called the North Atlantic Drift Current. The prevailing winds at that time of year are also from the southwest. Her track made good was probably pretty straight with no course changes and little or no tacking necessary to accomplish it.

of the shore, but we touched not, because the winde was faire, and we thought our selues sufficiently watered and wooded.[7]

Heere our Captaine obserued the sunne, and found himself in the latitude of 40 degrees and 7 minutes: so he iudged the North part of Cueruo to be in 40 degrees.[8]

After we had kept our course about a hundred leagues from the Ilands, by continuall Southerly windes we were forced and

---

[7] Captain Waymouth's reticence to expose his ship to piracy, or a possibly dangerous encounter, at Corvo is understandable, but his comfort with his level of stores and water after fourteen days at sea, especially considering the uncertainty of his destination, is remarkable. It is once again conjecture, but this would seem to indicate a vessel capable of carrying a much larger complement than he had, with attendant stores. We are given no information about the ship, but there was a ship named *Archangel*, 250 tons, in the fleet of Sir Anthony Sherley which, when Sherley met with the large fleet of the Earle of Essex at Plymouth bound for Cadiz in April 1596, he turned over to Essex for his use (Hakluyt, 1903). We have also found a privateer named *Archangel*, 265 tons, of London, Captain Michael Geare, in the Caribbean in 1602–03 (Andrews, April 1974, p. 250–52). There is no way to connect Waymouth's *Archangell* with either, except to say that Captain Geare and his ship were part of a privateering squadron under the command of Christopher Newport, who was well connected with the founders of the Virginia Company and was later made the admiral of Virginia. The actual owner of neither ship is known. It is not unlikely that these ships were one and the same.

[8] This statement shows the need by all sea captains to confirm their own calculations against a known landmark. This was not possible when voyaging in uncharted waters, making any confirmation of last known landfall very important. Captain Waymouth found his own latitude to be 40°7' north. He also observed the island about seven miles away.

driuen from the Southward, whither we first intended.[9] And when our Captaine by long beating saw it was but in vaine to striue with windes, not knowing Gods purposes heerin to our further blessing, (which after by his especiall direction wee found) he thought best to stand as nigh as he could by the winde to recouer what land we might first discouer.

Munday, the 6 of May, being in the latitude of 39 and a halfe about ten a clocke afore noone, we came to a riplin, which we discerned a head our ship, which is a breach of water caused either by a fall, or by some meeting of currents, which we iudged this to

[9] At this point the intent was to follow the same trackline he had been on, well to the southwest of the Azores. What cannot be known from this statement is how long he intended to follow this course, and what his new course would be. At any rate, his wind shifted into the southwest quadrant, requiring him to beat (tack alternately to port, then to starboard) into the wind and current, causing little net gain along his intended course. In fact, it is likely that the 100 leagues he did advance in that direction, before giving up, took more than 10 days.

His only reasonable alternative, and the one he took, was to go on the starboard tack, point his bow into the wind as much as would allow a reasonable headway without regard for a compass course, and sail that way until either a wind shift, or reaching land. Assuming he had reached latitude 36° north (100 leagues past Corvo on his original trackline), in all likelihood this would have resulted in a new westerly course along latitude 36° north.

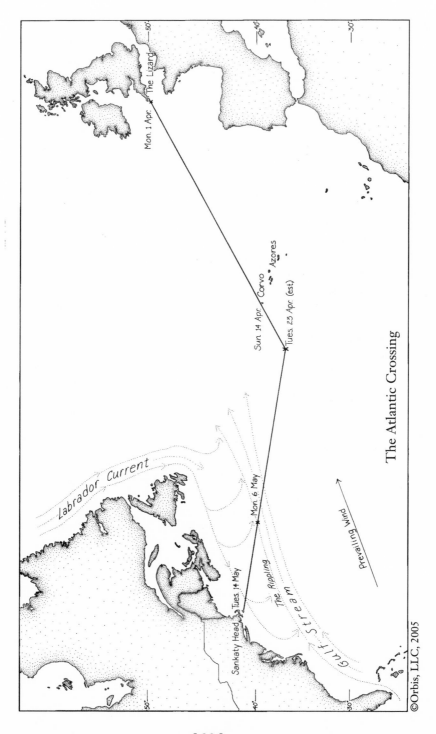

The Atlantic Crossing

The Lizard

Mon. 1 Apr.

Sun. 14 Apr. Corvo • Azores

Tues. 23 Apr. (est)

Labrador Current

Mon. 6 May

The Rippling

Gulf Stream

Sankaty Head Tues. 14 May

Prevailing Wind

©Orbis, LLC, 2005

be; for the weather being very faire, and a small gale of winde, we sounded and found no ground in a hundred fathoms.[10]

Munday, the 13 of May, about eleuen a clocke afore noon, our Captaine, iudging we were not farre from land, sounded, and

---

[10] The term rippling is still in use and one of the areas where the phenomenon is most dramatically demonstrated is along the west wall of the Gulf Stream where its northbound, warm water slides against the cold water of the southbound Labrador Current, where *Archangell* undoubtedly encountered it. Unfortunately, because the course and boundaries of these moving rivers are constantly changing there is no way to identify the exact location of their encounter. However, the latitude given, along with some reasonable assumptions, provides some insight into the trackline which was traversed from Corvo (see Chronology), and where *Archangell* would have made landfall, given the wind and currents which she encountered.

As Rosier has previously indicated, Captain Waymouth attempted to continue in a southwesterly direction past Corvo but managed to accomplish only about 300 miles that way. That would have put the ship in the general vicinity of latitude 36° north and longitude 34° west when the decision was made to fall off on the starboard tack, to the westward. Assuming they had made 1 knot per hour headway for the 300 miles, this leg of the voyage from Corvo would have taken twelve and one-half days, the course being changed in the early morning of 27 April. The prevailing winds at that latitude, at that time of year, would have been from the southwest, perhaps allowing them to steer due west. Their course made good (trackline) would be somewhat to the north of west due to the northerly setting effects of the wind and current, which would have increased as they approached the North American East Coast.

Captain Waymouth undoubtedly made a compromise between pointing as far into the south as possible, at a sacrifice of speed, and letting his bow fall off, making his landfall unacceptably far to the north. Such a course of action could easily have allowed 4.5 knots and caused him to be at latitude 39°30' north and longitude 60° west at ten in the morning on 6 May, where they observed the rippling.

had a soft oaze in a hundred and sixty fathomes. At fowre a clocke after noone we sounded againe, and had the same oaze in a hundred fathoms.[11]

From 10 a clocke that night till three a clocke in the morning, our Captaine tooke in all sailes and lay at hull, being desirous to fall with the land in the day time, because it was an vnknown coast, which it pleased God in his mercy to grant vs, otherwise we had run our ship vpon the hidden rockes and perished all. For when we set saile we sounded in 100 fathoms: and by eight a clocke, hauing not made aboue fiue or six leagues, our Captaine vpon a sudden change of water (supposing verily he saw the sand) presently sounded, and had but fiue fathoms. Much maruelling because we saw no land, he sent one to the top, who thence descried a whitish sandy cliffe, which bare West-North-West about six leagues from vs:[12] but comming neerer within three or fowre

[11] In five hours' time traveling at, perhaps, between 3 and 4 knots, they experienced shoaling from 160 fathoms to 100 fathoms. This could have occurred at several places in the Gulf of Maine north of Georges Bank. It is problematical, however. From any of those possible positions more than a day's sailing in a southerly direction against wind and current would have been required to reach a 5-fathom shoal with breakers, from which could be seen a high cliff. The other, and most likely possibility, is that *Archangell* crossed the continental shelf from the southeast at a point in the vicinity of Gilbert and Oceanographer Canyons, south of Georges Bank, where a diagonal traverse of the 500-fathom and 100-fathom curves would admit to the soundings stated and put the ship at latitude 40°27' north and longitude 68°8' west or 58 nautical miles southeast of the southeastrn extremity of Nantucket Shoals at four in the afternoon on 13 May.

[12] If Captain Waymouth continued, without deviation, from four in the afternoon till ten o'clock at night, the ship would have traveled into the Great South Channel, an area where up to 3-knot tidal currents would have affected her movements, whether sailing or lying ahull.

There can be little doubt that sometime around eight o'clock in the morning of 14 May the captain of *Archangell* found himself in an extremely precarious position in the middle of Davis Bank on Nantucket Shoals where Sankaty Head could be seen from the top, sixteen or eighteen miles distant.

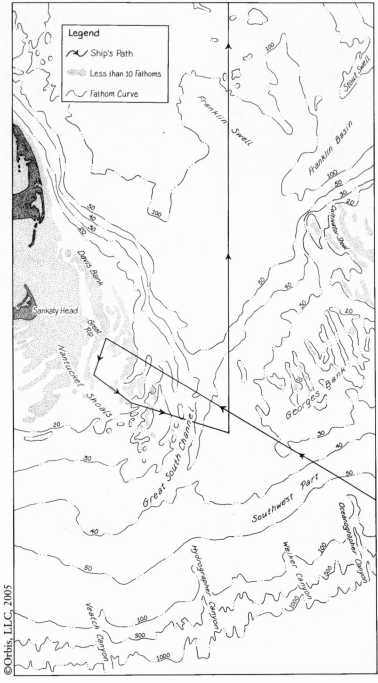

Legend

Ship's Path

Less than 10 Fathoms

Fathom Curve

Franklin Swell

Stout Swell

Franklin Basin

Davis Bank

Cultivator Shoal

Sankaty Head

Great Rip

Nantucket Shoals

Georges Bank

Great South Channel

Southwest Part

Oceanographer Canyon

Hydrographer Canyon

Welker Canyon

Veatch Canyon

The American Landfall

leagues, we saw many breaches still neerer the land: at last we espied a great breach a head vs al along the shore, into which before we should enter, our Captaine thought best to hoise out his ship boate and sound it. Which if he had not done, we had beene in great danger: for he bare vp the ship, as neere as he durst after the boat: Vntill Thomas Cam, his mate, being in the boat, called to him to tack about & stand off, for in this breach he had very showld water, two fathoms and lesse vpon the rockes, and sometime they supposed they saw the rocke within three or fowre foote, whereon the sea made a very strong breach: which we might discern (from the top) to run along as we sailed by it 6 or 7 leagues to the Southward. This was in the latitude of 41 degrees, 20 minuts: wherefore we were constrained to put backe again from the land:[13] and sounding, (the weather being very faire and a small winde) we found our selues embaied with continuall showldes and rockes in a most vncertaine ground, from five or sixe fathoms, at the next cast of the lead we should haue 15 & 18 fathoms. Ouer many which we passed, and God so blessed vs, that we had winde and weather as faire as poore men in this distresse could wish: whereby we both perfectly discerned every breach, and with the winde were able to turne, where we saw most hope of safest passage. Thus we parted from the land, which we had not as much before desired, and at the first sight reioiced, as now we all ioifully praised God, that it pleased him to deliuer vs from so imminent danger.

[13] This statement is perfectly descriptive of the Great Rip, a ridge of 1 to 5 fathoms' depth of water, about eighteen miles long.

Rosier states their position as latitude 41°20'. This position was probably determined at some point after disentangling themselves from the disastrous situation they were in, for it is difficult to imagine Captain Waymouth having the presence of mind or time at that point to be bothered with a sun sight. In any case, it probably describes their latitude position pretty accurately.

Heere we found great store of excellent Cod fish, and saw many whales, as we had done two or three daies before.

We stood off all that night, and the next day being Wednesday; but the winde still continuing between the points of South-South-West, and West-South-West: so as we could not make any way to the Southward, in regard of our great want of water and wood (which was now spent) we much desired land, and therefore sought for it, where the winde would best suffer vs to refresh ourselues.

Thursday the 16 of May, we stood in directly with the land, and much maruelled we descried it not, wherein we found our sea charts very false, putting land where none is.[14]

Friday the 17 of May, about six a clocke at night we descried the land, which bare from vs North-North-East; but because it blew a great gale of winde, the sea very high, and neere night, not fit to come vpon an vnknowen coast, we stood off till two a clocke

---

[14] Apparently, after narrowly escaping the breakers, when satisfied that the ship was out of danger, Captain Waymouth hove into the wind and tried to maintain his position until Wednesday morning. When he was convinced that he had little choice, he headed in a northeasterly direction, with the wind. This, of course, took the ship toward the center of the Gulf of Maine, so that on Thursday when he again hoped to find land by traveling in a northwesterly direction, it was much farther that way than he perceived.

It is, perhaps, worthwhile noting here that Waymouth, knowing his latitude, and having some sort of charts of the coast (no doubt based on information from his predecessors, Gosnold and Pring) in hand, made a concerted effort to go in a direction that would take him below that latitude. This, in addition to his earlier effort to sail southward from the Azores, would seem to confirm a clear indication that his intended destination was not the Maine Coast.

in the morning, being Saturday:[15] then standing in with it againe, we descried it by eight a clocke in the morning, bearing North-East from vs. It appeared a meane high land, as we after found it, being but an iland of some six miles in compasse, but I hope the most fortunate euer discouered. About twelue a clocke that day, we came to an anker on the North side of this iland, about a league from the shore. About two a clocke our Captaine with twelue men rowed in his ship-boat to the shore, where we made no long stay, but laded our boat with dry wood of olde trees vpon the shore side, and returned to our ship, where we rode that night.[16]

This Iland is woody, growen with Firre, Birch, Oke and Beech, as farre as we saw along the shore; and so likely to be within. On the verge grow Gooseberries, Strawberries, Wild pease, and Wild-rose bushes. The water issued foorth downe the rocky cliffes in many places: and much fowle of diuers kinds breed vpon the shore and rocks.

While we were at shore, our men aboord with a few hooks got aboue thirty great Cods and Haddocks, which gaue vs a taste of the great plenty of fish which we found afterward wheresoeuer we went vpon the coast.

[15] It is doubtful that Rosier here refers to a storm when he refers to "a great gale of winde." Although it is not at all unusual to have a storm in May on the Maine Coast, with attendant easterly winds, the conditions to which he no doubt refers are gusty southwest winds with choppy seas. Captain Waymouth is exercising more caution than he had when first making landfall at Nantucket. Here we see exercised one of the cardinal rules of shiphandling for sailing ships, especially the cumbersome square-rigged ships of Waymouth's time: never allow the vessel to be put on a lee shore if sailing into the wind is required to get back off, especially so if it is an unfamiliar shore, in darkness. Upon reaching land at Nantucket Shoals the wind, being southwest, had been on the ship's beam, allowing for maneuverability, and a certain lack of caution.

[16] The "fortunate" island, of course, was Monhegan. That Waymouth was comfortable leaving his ship at anchor in an unprotected road, on an unknown coast to help get firewood is probably indicative of the trust he placed in his crew. Even so, he did no exploring, apparently staying no longer than absolutely necessary.

From hence we might discerne the maine land from the West-South-West to the East-North-East, and a great way (as it then seemed, and as we after found it) up into the maine we might discern very high mountaines, though the maine seemed but low land;[17] which gaue vs a hope it would please God to direct vs to the discouery of some good; although wee were driuen by winds farre from that place, whither (both by our direction and desire) we euer intended to shape the course of our voyage.[18]

The next day, being Whit-Sunday; because we rode too much open to the sea and windes, we weyed anker about twelue a clocke, and came along to the other ilands more adioyning to the

[17] Since the view inland from high on Monhegan is not discernably different than that at sea level, twelve miles from the coast, there would have been no need to seek a high vantage point. Rosier has also stated that the shore party did not go inland on the island, something they would have had to do to get a high vantage point, aside from scaling cliffs. It seems reasonable to conclude, therefore, that his use of the term "From hence" refers to the general vicinity of the ship at anchor and on the shore of Monhegan.

"Very high mountains" at first seems to imply something other than the hills at Camden, Hope, and Union, or a serious exaggeration. There is no doubt that what James Rosier saw were those same hills. However, perhaps exaggeration is unfair. These hills do, in fact, stand out in contrast to the low-lying country around them. Also, it should be remembered that this is only the impression of the observer, a man who had seen nothing higher than the horizon at sea for a month. Rosier also seems to have been an academic, not jaded by worldly experience who, rightly, was impressed by nearly everything he saw in this New World.

[18] Once again Rosier confirms that their original destination was well below the latitude of their landfall at Nantucket.

maine, and in the rode directly with the mountaines, about three leagues from the first iland where we ankered.[19]

When we came neere unto them (sounding all along in a good depth) our Captaine manned his ship-boat and sent her before with Thomas Cam one of his mates, whom he knew to be of good experience, to sound and search between the ilands for a place safe for our shippe to ride in; in the meane while we kept aloofe at sea, hauing giuen them in the boat a token to weffe in the ship, if he found a conuenient harbour;[20] which it pleased God to send vs, farre beyond our expectation, in a most safe birth de-

[19] By mid May the summer southwesterly winds prevail in the Gulf of Maine, as Waymouth had already learned. They tend to be strongest in the afternoon and if he was anchored a full league from Monhegan he had no protection, perhaps explaining why he began to feel uncomfortable and sought a better anchorage around noon. The Georges Islands— Allen, Benner, Burnt, and Little Burnt—all lie in the "rode" (a direct line) between Monhegan and the Camden Hills, and are about six miles from Monhegan.

[20] Cam, an experienced and well-qualified seaman, while satisfying himself of a safe anchorage for *Archangell*, would have considered, seriously, a safe entrance, as well, before signaling the captain to follow him in. The channel between Allen and Burnt Islands would have made him cautious—the entrance to the channel lies directly exposed to the southwest, where, in a southwest breeze there can be considerable surge and wind chop. In any but a northerly wind the channel at the southern ends of Allen and Burnt Islands would be considered a lee shore, prompting extreme caution by any sailing master of that time. The channel, however, has almost 10 fathoms of water along the Burnt Island shore and if Cam was assured that there were no obstacles near areas sounded and that the ship could stay in the deepest part of the channel with wind astern, he would certainly have chosen it, especially considering the natural harbor just inside. Soundings to the north of the Dry Ledges, between Burnt Island and Allen Island, would have shown a wide area of relatively flat bottom in 60 feet of water. It would have been in the lee of the Dry Ledges, as well.

fended from all windes, in an excellant depth of water for ships of any burthen, in six, seuen, eight, nine, and ten fathoms vpon a clay oaze very tough.[21] We all with great ioy praised God for his vnspeakable goodnesse, who had from so apparent danger deliuered vs, & directed vs vpon this day into so secure an Harbour: in remembrance whereof we named it Pentecost-harbour, we arriuing there that day out of our last Harbour in England, from whence we set saile vpon Easterday.

[21] "Safe birth defended from all windes," although essentially true for all but northerly winds, illustrates a certain naiveté which is characteristic of Rosier's narrative from here onward, which begs the point that it was then spring in Maine (ten days must be added to Rosier's Julian dates to understand the season by our present-day Gregorian calendar), and for the remainder of their stay they were observing better and better summer weather under the best conditions Maine has to offer to seafarers in a good summer.

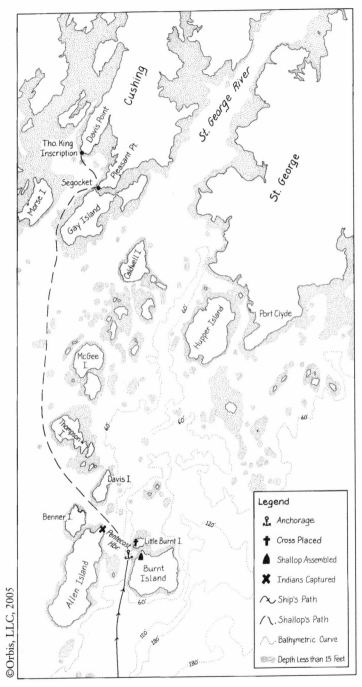

Cushing

St. George River

St. George

Davis Point

Tho. King
Inscription

Pleasant Pt.

Segocket

Morse I.

Gay Island

Caldwell I.

Hupper Island

Port Clyde

60'

McGee
I.

Thompson
I.

60'

60'

60'

Davis I.

Benner I.

120'

Pentecost
Hbr.

Little Burnt I.

Allen Island

Burnt
Island

60'

120'

180'

180'

Legend

⚓ Anchorage

✝ Cross Placed

🔺 Shallop Assembled

✖ Indians Captured

〰 Ship's Path

∧ Shallop's Path

∿ Bathymetric Curve

░ Depth Less than 15 Feet

Pentecost Harbor

About foure a clocke, after we were ankered and well mored,[22] our Captaine with halfe a dozen of our company went on shore to seeke fresh watering, and a conuenient place to set to-

[22] Much has been said about the possible specific location of *Archangell*'s mooring and what area Waymouth and Rosier considered to be Pentecost Harbor. This writer's view holds that an area of about one-half mile in diameter, bounded by Burnt and Little Burnt Islands on the east, Allen Island on the west, and the Dry Ledges on the south, constitutes a large deep harbor which is greatly protective in easterly, south-westerly, and westerly winds, and has a good holding bottom at depths fitting Rosier's description. Later in the narrative Rosier will state that the Dry Ledges lie at the entrance to the harbor.

The time required to weigh anchor at Monhegan, sail to Burnt Island, and moor securely in the harbor would have meant little of the four hours was taken for searching and sounding. Cam, entering the harbor through the opening on the southwest of Burnt Island in the ship's boat, would have immediately found himself in the lee of the Dry Ledges with a choice of good mooring places having 60 feet of water on good holding bottom nearly against any shore. This would supply their immediate need for a protected anchorage, and upon closer inspection, the longer-term need for required shore activities. Of course these activities required some reasonably level ground or beach area, whereby visual and audible communication could be maintained between ship and shore. These requirements could only have been met at the northwest point of Burnt Island just above the sand beach.

The practice of anchoring and mooring involved setting the ship's anchor offshore and mooring the ship to a fixed object (or objects, depending on the number of lines used) on the shore, keeping tension on the anchor cable. This practice kept the anchor chain (or rope cable) from twisting with tide changes and confined the ship to a limited space. Because Rosier tells us that the ship was moored, the shore chosen for the stern hawser would almost certainly have been on Little Burnt Island. That would have placed the ship in a position headed into any southerly wind funneling up through the harbor, with its broad side facing the beach, for guns to bear, in the event of any trouble ashore. It was also close enough to the shore for communication and for easy boat traffic to and from shore activities.

gether a pinnesse, which we brought in pieces out of England: both which we found very fitting.[23]

[23] Groundwater wells can be dug on almost any island on the coast of Maine having topsoil with clay beneath it. Burnt Island being about 300 acres in size, almost completely covered with topsoil and vegetation, and having a good slope from 135 feet to sea level, has many ideal places for groundwater wells, like those Rosier describes.

The shallop is here called a pinnace, which may be some indication of its size. It must have been a marvelous piece of kit construction, sure to invite the envy of today's wooden boat enthusiasts. In this case it was large enough to be rowed and sailed effectively by eight men with the weight of at least seventeen men, some with armor, aboard. Such a craft could have been up to 35 feet in length and weigh 10 tons, probably more if any scarce English oak was used. In the English Caribbean privateering period of 1585–1604 shallops were used heavily as small, highly manueverable fighting platforms. They had their own crews and were independent of the larger ships in their squadrons, often taking on very large Spanish ships by themselves—and prevailing. They were, however, too large to be carried by a ship and had to be towed or make ocean voyages on their own. In spite of their size, they were usually rowed by only eight men, four on a side. Many were constructed in England, dismantled part by part, and carried in the hold of their mother ship, in this case *Archangell*, in pieces. No doubt there was a small industry in Europe centered around building the kits for these small, necessary vessels of the period. England's forests were depleted and it is known that such boat kits were also imported from Norway. The fact that it could be put together, caulked, and fitted out in nine days is further proof that it had been assembled previously, or that the pieces were at least cut from uniform patterns, and that the carpenter, with what skills he no doubt possessed, only required the help of the cooper and laborers to put it together.

Vpon this Iland, as also vpon the former, we found (at our first comming to shore) where fire had beene made: and about the place were very great egge shelles bigger than goose egges, fish bones, and as we iudged, the bones of some beast.

Heere we espied Cranes stalking on the shore of a little Iland adioyning;[24] where we after saw they vsed to breed.

Whitsun-munday, the 20 day of May, very early in the morning, our Captaine caused the pieces of the pinnesse to be carried ashore, where while some busied about her, others digged welles to receiue the fresh water, which we found issuing downe out of the land in many places. Heere I can not omit (for foolish feare of imputation of flattery) the painfull industry of our Captaine, who as at sea he is alwayes most carefull and vigilant, so at land he refuseth no paines; but his labour was euer as much or rather more than any mans: which not only encourageth others with better content, but also effecteth much with great expedition.[25]

In digging we found excellent clay for bricke or tile. The next day we finished a well of good and holesome cleere water in a great empty caske, which we left there.[26] We cut yards, waste

[24] The term adjoining is used several times in the narrative of events taking place near the ship. The little island is Little Burnt Island, which is literally adjoining Burnt Island. If the shoreside mooring cable were fastened on the shore on the west side of Little Burnt Island, next to the sand beach, it would have been adjoining the ship, as well. At this anchorage location there are 70 feet of water right at the sand beach on the Burnt Island shore.

[25] Captain Waymouth seems to accomplish much with leadership by example, as indicated throughout the narrative. Perhaps it is simply Rosier's enthusiasm, but there seems to be much volunteerism, camaraderie, and freedom of movement shown by the crew, indicating a competent leadership style. In an adventure such as this, teamwork was absolutely necessary to basic survival, perhaps explaining why many voyages of discovery were disastrous.

[26] The digging of wells to collect groundwater is one indication that the brook on Allen Island had not yet been discovered.

trees, and many necessaries for our ship, while our Carpenter and Cooper laboured to fit and furnish forth the shallop.[27]

This day our boat went about a mile from our ship, and in small time with two or three hooks was fished sufficiently for our whole company three dayes, with great Cod, Haddocke, and Thornebacke.

And towards night we drew with a small net of twenty fathoms very nigh the shore: we got about thirty very good and great Lobsters, many Rockfish, some plaise, and other small fishes called Lumpes, verie pleasant to the taste: and we generally obserued, that all the fish, of what kind soeuer we tooke, were well fed, fat, and sweet in taste.

Wednesday, the 22 of May, we felled and cut wood for our ships use, cleansed and scoured our wels, and digged a plot of ground, wherein, amongst some garden seeds, we sowed peaze and barley, which in sixteen dayes grew eight inches aboue ground; and so continued growing euery day halfe an inch, although this was but the crust of the ground, and much inferior to the mould we after found in the maine.

Friday, the 24 of May, after we had made an end to cutting wood, and carrying water aboord our shippe, with fourteen shot and pikes we marched about and thorow part of two of the ilands; the bigger of which we iudged to be foure or fiue miles in compasse, and a mile broad.[28]

[27] Cutting yards, waist trees, and other necessaries for the ship, as well as collecting water and firewood, all basic necessities for survival, must have been drudgery when an exotic new land beckoned. But the orderly way in which their activities were planned and carried out shows the instinctive discipline necessary to a good seaman of the time.

[28] Since their activities to now had been confined to Burnt Island, and those activities would have meant a reasonably complete inspection of it, the islands referred to here would be Allen and Benner. These are adjacent to one another and it would be natural to explore each from the same starting point in the little gut that runs between them.

The profits and fruits which are naturally on these Ilands are these:

All along the shore and some space within, where the wood hindereth not, grow plentifully.	Rasberries. Gooseberries. Strawberries. Roses. Currants. Wild-vines. Angelica.
Within the Ilands growe wood of sundry sorts, some very great, and all tall:	Birch. Beech. Ash. Maple. Spruce. Cherry-tree. Yew. Oke very great and good.

Firre-tree, out of which issueth Turpentine in so maruellous plenty, and so sweet, as our Chirurgeon and others affirmed they neuer saw so good in England. We pulled off much Gumme congealed on the outside of the barke, which smelled like Frankincense. This would be a great benefit for making Tarre and Pitch.[29]

---

[29] Here is a good description of spruce gum, highly esteemed by children of the nineteenth century as a chewing gum. Although the turpentine must have been evaporated to a great extent from the gum, one has to wonder about its effect when taken internally.

We stayed the longer in this place, not only because of our good harbour (which is an excellent comfort) but because euery day we did more and more discouer the pleasant fruitfulnesse; insomuch as many of our Companie wished themselues setled heere, not expecting any farther hopes, or better discouery to be made.[30]

Heere our men found abundance of great muscels among the rocks; and in some of them many small Pearls: and in one Muscell (which we drew vp in our net) was found foureteene Pearles, whereof one of prety bignesse and orient: in another aboue fiftie small Pearles: and if we had a drag, no doubt we had found some of great valew, seeing these did certainly shew, that heere they were bred: the shels all glistering with mother of Pearle.

Wednesday, the 29 day, our shallop now being finished, and our Captaine and men furnished to depart with hir from the ship: we set vp a crosse on the shore side vpon the rockes.[31]

[30] Once again we get an indication that this was not the part of the American coast that was originally sought, but that they believed they had found a place just as good. One can't help but speculate about how things might have been different if a small dose of early November weather were introduced at this point. Rosier, and even Waymouth himself, apparently had no concept of winter weather conditions on this part of the Atlantic Coast at this latitude. There had been no experience in winter this far north of Roanoke and knowledge of adverse conditions in the Newfoundland fishery and northward could be explained by the much higher latitude. In any case, it seems they were oblivious to the possibility of any climate other than what they were experiencing. As a result, could the naive enthusiasm of this narrative have contributed in any way to the unrealistic expectations and ultimate failure of the Popham Colony two years later?

[31] "Upon the shore side vpon the rockes" could describe almost any place around the harbor, but for a ship entering by the channel from the south, as Cam had, the most prominent place for the cross to be seen by all seafarers who entered would have been well above the high tide mark on the west point of Little Burnt Island.

Thursday, the 30 of May, about ten a clocke afore noon, our Captaine with 13 men more, in the name of God, and with all our praiers for their prosperous discouery, and safe returne, departed in the shallop: leaving the ship in a good harbour, which before I mentioned, well mored, and manned with 14 men. This day, about fiue a clocke in the afternoon, we in the shippe espied three canoas comming towards vs, which went to the iland adioyning, where they went a shore, and very quickly made a fire, about which they stood beholding our ship:[32] to whom we made signes with our hands and hats, weffing vnto them to come vnto vs, because we had not seene any of the people yet. They sent one Canoa with three men, one of which, when they came neere vnto vs, spake in his language very lowd and very boldly: seeming as though he would know why we were there, and by pointing with this oare towards the sea, we coniectured he meant we should be gone. But when we shewed them kniues and their vse by cutting of stickes and other trifles, as combs and glasses, they came close aboard our ship, as desirous to entertain our friendship. To these we gaue such things as we perceiued they liked, when we shewed them the vse: bracelets, rings, peacocke-feathers, which they stucke in their haire, and Tabacco pipes. After their departure to their company on the shore, presently came foure other in a Canoa: to whom we gaue as to the former, vsing them with as much kindnes as we could.

[32] Once again Rosier refers to the "iland adioyning," but here omits "little." This again might appear to be Burnt or Little Burnt Island. However, there are strong indications at several places in the narrative that the island adjoining which was used as a base for Indian activities was Allen Island, and that the place where they had fires and observed the ship's activities from a high vantage point was the northeast point of the island. *Archangell*'s position at Little Burnt Island would have allowed the ship's crew to observe any canoes coming toward them from that location.

The shape of their body is very proportionable, they are well countenanced, not very tal nor big, but in stature like to vs: they paint their bodies with blacke, their faces, some with red, some with blacke, and some with blew.

Their clothing is Beauers skins, or Deares skins, cast ouer them like a mantle, and hanging downe to their knees, made fast together vpon the shoulder with leather: some of them had sleeues, most had none: some had buskins of such leather tewed: they haue besides a peece of Beauers skin between their legs, made fast about their waste, to couer their priuities.

They suffer no haire to grow on their faces, but on their head very long and very blacke, which those that haue wiues, binde vp behinde with a leather string, in a long round knot.

They seem all very ciuill and merrie: shewing tokens of much thankfulnesse, for those things we gaue them. We found them then (as after) a people of exceeding good inuention, quicke and vnderstanding and readie capacitie.

Their Canoas are made without any iron, of the bark of a Birch tree, strengthened within with ribs and hoops of wood, in so good fashion, with such excellent ingenious art, as they are able to beare seuen or eight persons, far exceeding any in the Indies. One of their Canoas came not to us wherein we imagined their women were:[33] of whom they are (as all Saluages) very jealous.

---

[33] Rosier here indicates that the occupants of the third canoe which was seen coming, initially, could not be identified and speculates that it contained women. The inference taken here is that the canoes were seen coming from a distance and went to the island adjoining, not being close enough for the occupants to be identified (it was about a third of a mile from the ship at the Little Burnt Island side of the harbor to the northeast point of Allen Island). Two of the canoes came to the ship, one at a time, and the occupants of the third (whether women or not) remained at the fire where they could see but not easily be seen.

When I signed vnto them they should goe sleepe, because it was night, they vnderstood presently, and pointed at the shore, right against our ship, they would stay all night:[34] as they did.

The next morning very early, came one canoa abord vs againe with three saluages, whom we easily then enticed into our ship, and vnder deck:[35] where we gaue them porke, fish, bread and pease, all which they did eat: and this I noted, they would eat nothing raw, either fish or flesh. They maruelled much and much looked vpon the making of our canne and kettle, so they did at a head-peece and at our guns, of which they were most fearefull, and would fall flat downe at the report of them. At their departure I signed vnto them, that if they would bring me such skins as they ware I would giue them kniues, and such things as I saw they most liked, which the chiefe of them promised to do by that time the Sunne should be beyond the middest of the firmament;[36] this I

---

[34] It appears that one canoe with three Indians went back to join the others, presumably near their fireside on Allen Island. When four of those who had not gone to the ship realized what gifts they had missed, they presently took one canoe to get their share of the spoils. These four, when asked to leave, pointed at the place where they intended to camp for the night, "at the shore, right against our ship." The place would probably have been on or above the sand beach. Rosier's concept of sleeping arrangements included frame houses, inns, etc. It did not include sleeping in the open, on a rocky shore, under the stars. He apparently expected the Natives to return to their "houses" on the mainland some distance away.

[35] Here we have a canoe with three natives arriving at the ship early in the morning and no mention of the others who had camped nearby the night before. Throughout the narrative canoes with Natives seem to come and go, independent of each other.

[36] The spokesman has promised to bring furs and skins for trade with Rosier by noon. This would confirm that the three canoes had come the previous afternoon either out of curiosity or to fish and hunt, and had nothing in their canoes which could be used for trade. It also would indicate that they had access to furs and skins for trade within a distance of something around four hours round trip. They almost certainly came from a village located on a point of land at the west end of Pleasant Point Gut which separates the Cushing peninsula and Gay Island.

did bring to them an vnderstanding of exchange, and that they might conceiue the intent of our comming to them to be for no other end.[37]

About 10 a clocke this day we descried our Shallop returning towards vs, which so soon as we espied, we certainly coniectured our Captaine had found some vnexpected harbour, further up towards the maine to bring the ship into, or some riuer; knowing his determination and resolution, not so suddenly else to make return:[38] which when they came neerer they expressed by shooting volleies of shot, they gaue vs a volley and haled vs, then we in the shippe gaue them a great peece and haled them.

Thus we welcomed them, who gladded vs exceedingly with their ioyful relation of their happie discouery, which shall appeare in the sequele. And we likewise gaue them cause of mutuall ioy with vs, in discoursing of the kinde ciuility we found in a people, where we little expected any sparke of humanity.[39]

---

[37] It seems a bit naive to think that these people had no understanding of exchange, at the same time expecting that a store of surplus goods would be available for the purpose. We might see here the first indication that Rosier was being coy and beginning to hatch a plan for the eventual kidnapping of some of them.

[38] From this remark it is obvious that Waymouth intended to be gone longer than a day. Apparently the opportunity to move his ship, safely, closer to these mountains which had been beckoning, along with his ability to move swiftly with the tides, prompted him to hurry back.

[39] Here we see the roles that Rosier and Waymouth played throughout this adventure, and the strengths of each man's interest. Waymouth is returning from a small and perhaps dangerous voyage of discovery, wherein he had covered new ground and seen new places, with the prospect of a good habitation site, something his backers required from this voyage. Rosier, as an academic, has made a fascinating discovery of a new people, their language, customs, morals, and intelligence—enough to keep him busy for some time with research and writing. Here we really see Rosier's delight and keen interest in these people. At this point one can almost read his mind; these people, far from being the unintelligent hostile savages he had expected, could now be seen as knowlegeable, friendly Natives with much information to be exploited regarding the state of their country.

Our Captaine had in this small time discouered up a great riuer, trending alongst into the maine about forty miles. The pleasantnesse whereof, with the safety of harbour for shipping, together with the fertility of ground and other fruits, which were generally by his whole company related, I omit, till I report of the whole discouery therein after performed.[40] For by the breadth, depth and strong flood, imagining it to run far vp into the land, he with speed returned, intending to flanke his light horsman for arrowes, least it might happen that the further part of the riuer should be narrow, and by that meanes subiect to the volley of Saluages on either side out of the woods.[41]

Vntil his returne, our Captaine left on shoare where he landed in a path (which seemed to be frequented) a pipe, a brooch and a knife, thereby to know if the Saluages had recourse that way, because they could at that time see none of them, but they were

[40] It is at this point in the narrative that the great controversy surrounding Waymouth's voyage has been waged. The issue concerns why Rosier would have described traveling some forty miles into the St. George River, which is not safely navigable by a vessel like *Archangell*, and only navigable by the shallop for, perhaps, twelve miles. It should also be clearly understood that from the anchorage at Georges Islands, the St. George River cannot be seen, nor can the area around Huppers Island be identified as the mouth of a river. Without prior knowledge of the geography of the area, Waymouth would not even have known it existed and it is certain that the St. George had not been discovered prior to Waymouth's arrival. On the other hand, the existence of Penobscot Bay and its proximity to the Camden Hills is obvious from Monhegan. With that in mind, all further references to the river in the notes will assume the Penobscot River to be the river in question.

[41] This is the first reference in the narrative of the shallop as a Light Horseman. It is no coincidence that it will not be called a shallop or pinnace again. For here he puts armor on it and mans it with armed soldiers. The term *Light Horseman* emphasizes its military importance in addition to its being a watercraft.

taken away before our returne thither.[42] I returne noe to our Saluages, who according to their appointment about one a clocke,
came with 4 Canoas to the shoare of the Iland right ouer against
vs, where they had lodged the last night, and sent one Canoa to vs
with two of those Saluages, who had beene a bord, and another,
who then seemed to haue command of them: for though we perceiued their willingnesse, yet he would not permit them to come
abord: but he hauing viewed vs and our ship, signed that he would
go to the rest of the company and returne againe.[43] Presently after
their departure it began to raine, and continued all that afternoone, so as they could not come to vs with their skins and furs,
nor we go to them. But after an howre or there about, the three
which had beene with vs before came againe, whom we had to our
fire and couered them with our gownes. Our Captaine bestowed a
shirt vpon him, whom we thought to be their chiefe, who seemed
neuer to haue seene any before; we gaue him a brooch to hang
about his necke, a great knife, and lesser knives to the two other,
and to euery one of them a combe and glasse, the vse whereof we
shewed them: whereat they laughed and tooke gladly; we vict-

[42] The path, here mentioned, could have been any one of hundreds
in the Penobscot Bay area, which were, along with the ocean, rivers, and
streams, literally the highway system of the Native inhabitants. Because
Rosier states that they returned to it, the implication is that it was somewhere along their later route up the river, obviously beyond where the
ship stopped twenty-six miles up (i.e., somewhere between Jameson
Point in Rockport and Fort Point in Stockton Springs). Based on their
later shore exploration, this would seem to be somewhere in the vicinity
of Ogier Point, at the line between Rockport and Camden.

[43] The Natives who had promised skins for trade return, as Rosier
notes, by appointment. The difference seems to be that this time they
are accompanied by a man who is obviously in charge, perhaps a sagamore whose control of community property, such as a quantity of pelts,
would have required his presence during any trading session.

ualled them, and gaue them aqua vitae,[44] which they tasted, but would by no meanes drinke; our beuerage they liked well,[45] we gaue them Sugar Candy, which after they had tasted they liked and desired more, and raisons which were giuen them; and some of euery thing they would reserue to carry to their company. Wherefore we pittying their being in raine, and therefore not able to get themselues victuall (as we thought) we gaue them bread and fish.

Thus because we found the land a place answerable to the intent of our discouery, viz, fit for any nation to inhabit, we vsed the people with as great kindnes as we could deuise, or found them capable of.[46]

The next day, being Saturday and the first of Iune, I traded with the Saluages all the fore-noone vpon the shore, where were eight and twenty of them: and because our ship rode nigh, we were but fiue or sixe:[47] where for knives, glasses, combes and other trifles to the valew of foure or fiue shillings, we had 40 good Beauers skins, Otters skins, Sables, and other small skins, which we knew not how to call. Our trade being ended, many of them came abord vs, and did eat by our fire, and would be verie merrie and

[44] An English hard liquor or grain alcohol of the time. It is probably no wonder that the Abenaki didn't like this liquid. Good taste can't have been one of its redeeming values. Fortunately, they knew nothing of its effect at that point.

[45] Perhaps a malt beverage like beer. Perhaps cider. Perhaps some combination like posset, a popular drink of the time, made from hot milk, liquor, and spices (without the milk, unless they had a cow, of course).

[46] Once again Rosier indicates the purpose of the voyage—to discover a land fit for men of "any nation to inhabit."

[47] Here we have another indication that the ship was very close to the shore, giving Rosier some comfort while in the presence of so many natives. This is the only occasion where formal trade was conducted with the Indians. At all other times it seems that they had little with which to barter, indicating further that individuals either were not empowered to do any trading, or that all pelts and skins were community property. It might also be significant that there were twenty-eight Indians present, the largest number present near the harbor at any one time during the ship's stay.

bold, in regard of our kinde vsage of them. Towards night our Captaine went on shore, to haue a draught with the Sein or net. And we carried two of them with vs, who maruelled to see vs catch fish with a net.[48] Most of that we caught we gaue them and their company. Then on the shore I learned the names of diuers things of them: and when they perceiued me to note them down, they would of themselues, fetch fishes, and fruit bushes, and stand by me to see me write their names. Our Captaine shewed them a strange thing which they wondered at. His sword and mine hauing beene touched with the Loadstone,[49] tooke vp a knife, and held it fast when they plucked it away, made the knife turne, being laid on a blocke, and touching it with his sword, made that take vp a needle, whereat they much maruelled. This we did to cause them to imagine some great power in vs: and for that to loue and feare vs.

[48] The "sein or net" here was probably not much different than the purse seine used in the herring fishery today, where one side floats while the other sinks, the ends then being drawn around the school of fish to entrap them. The modern purse seine has a draw-string on the bottom edge which is drawn or pursed, preventing escape of fish from the bottom, allowing it to be used in any depth of water. The seine net used by Waymouth had no draw-string, requiring it to be set off a beach area in a depth of water about equal to the depth of the net. It was then drawn to the shore, ends first, with the bottom of the net touching bottom preventing escape of anything in its path. Because at the time there was such an abundance of bottom fish, lobsters, and molusks, such a method would have been extremely productive. However, a difficulty would have been any bottom irregularity or large rock that might snag the net as it was pulled in. For that reason the only location among the Georges Islands which would have permitted this kind of fishing would have been the sand beach cove where the old lifeboat station on Burnt Island is today.

[49] A natural magnet kept aboard every ship of the time for maintenance of the compass.

When we went on shore to trade with them, in one of their Canoas I saw their bowes and arrowes, which I tooke vp and drew an arrow in one of them, which I found to be of strength able to carry an arrow fiue or sixe score stronglie: and one of them tooke it and drew as we draw our bowes, not like the Indians. Their bow is made of Wich Hazell, and some of Beech in fashion much like our bowes, but they want nocks, onely a string of leather put through a hole at one end, and made fast with a knot at the other. Their arrowes are made of the same wood, some of Ash, big and long, with three feathers tied on, and nocked very artificiallie: headed with the long shanke bone of a Deere, made very sharpe with two fangs in manner of a harping iron. They haue likewise Darts, headed with like bone, one of which I darted among the rokes, and brake it not. These they vse very cunningly, to kill fish, fowle and beasts.

Our Captaine had two of them at supper with vs in his cabbin to see their demeanure, and had them in presence at service: who behaued themselues very ciuilly, neither laughing nor talking all the time, and at supper fed not like men of rude education, neither would they eat or drinke more than seemed to content nature; they desired pease to carry a shore to their women, which we gaue them, with fish and bread, and lent them pewter dishes, which they carefully brought againe.

In the euening another boat came to them on the shore, and because they had some Tabacco, which they brought for their own vse, the other came for vs, making signe what they had, and offered to carry some of vs in their boat, but foure or fiue of vs went with them in our owne boat: when we came on shore they gaue vs the best welcome they could, spreading fallow Deeres skins for vs to sit on the ground by their fire, and gaue vs of their Tabacco in our pipes which was excellent, and so generally commended of vs all to be as good as any we euer tooke, being the simple leafe without any composition, strong, and of sweet taste: they gaue vs some to carry to our Captaine, whom they called our Bashebes:[50] neither did they require any thing for it, but we would not receiue any thing from them without remuneration.

Heere we saw foure of their women, who stood behind them, as desirous to see vs, but not willing to be seene: for before, whensoeuer we came on shore, they retired into the woods, whether it were in regarde of their owne naturall modestie, being couered only as the men with the foresaid Beauers skins, or by the commanding iealously of their husbands, which we rather suspected, because it is an inclination much noted to be in Saluages; wherefore we would by no meanes seeme to take any speciall notice of them. They were well fauoured in proportion of countenance, though coloured blacke, low of stature, and fat, bare headed as the men, wearing their haire long: they had two little male children of a yeere and a halfe old, as we iudged, very fat and of good countenances, which they loue tenderly, all naked, except their legs, which were couered with thin leather buskins tewed, fastened with strops to a girdle about their waste, which they gird very straight, and is decked round about with little peeces of red Copper; to these I gaue chaines and bracelets, glasses, and other trifles which the Saluages seemed to accept in great kindnesse.

[50] The remark by Rosier, "our Captaine whom they called our Bashebes," confirms the traditional view that the term referred to a title, rather than a proper noun name. The term has been recently translated and found to have two roots in the Abnaki dialect. The first, *Pe'zek8*, represents the word "one," as in "only one" or "one only." When contracted in speech and with the *P* sounding like *B* this becomes *Be'*. The second element is *tzibagh* which translates to "greatest" synonymous with "most extraordinary." The roots combined are *Be'-tzibagh*, which translates to Basheba, "He who is the greatest one."

At our comming away, we would haue had those two that supped with vs, to go abord and sleepe, as they had promised: but it appeared their company would not suffer them. Whereat we might easily perceiue they were much greeued: but not long after our departure, they came with three more to our ship, signing to vs, that if one of our company would go lie on shore with them, they would stay with vs. Then Owen Griffin (one of the two we were to leaue in the Countrey, if we had thought it needfull or conuenient) went with them in their Canoa, and 3 of them staied abord vs, whom our whole company very kindly vsed.[51] Our Captaine saw their lodging prouided, and them lodged in an old saile vpon the Orlop:[52] and because they much feared our dogs, they were tied vp whensoeuer any of them came abord vs.[53]

Owen Griffin, which lay on the shore, reported vnto me their maner, and (as I may terme them) the ceremonies of their idolatry: which they performe thus. One among them (the eldest of the company as he iudged) riseth right vp, the other sitting still, and looking about, suddenly cried with a loud voice, baugh,

---

[51] This is the first mention of swapping one or two men as hostages. The practice apparently was devised by this small group to solve a difficult social dilemma; they had received an invitation which their manners and customs would dictate that they accept, but their caution was too great. This situation indicates a great deal of social advancement, and the ingenious solution shows clearly the ability of the Native American to practice diplomacy (ironically, this trait eventually contributed to his downfall). Owen Griffin apparently had signed on for the voyage in an agreement with Thomas Arundel, whereby he would stay in America if asked to (Purchas, *Pilgrims*, 1662, XIII, 1905, p. 344). It is difficult to understand such an arrangement but we will probably never know Griffin's reasoning for such bravado or what he thought he was destined for.

[52] A phonetic shortening of the word *overlap* which referred to a lower deck area of the vessel. The term *orlap* is still in use.

[53] It was not unusual for dogs to be carried on ships of the time. Two mastiffs were carried on the Pring voyage of 1603 and had been found, on at least one occasion, to be an effective deterrant against aggressive behavior on the part of a large number of Native Americans. It is possible that they were carried here as a result of that experience.

waugh: then the women fall down, and lie vpon the ground, and the men all together answering the same, fall a stamping round about the fire with both feet, as hard as they can making the ground shake, with sundry out-cries, and change of voice and sound. Many take the fire-sticks and thrust them into the earth, and then rest awhile: of a sudden beginning as before, they continue so stamping, til the yonger sort fetched from the shore many stones, of which euery man tooke one, and first beat vpon them with their fire sticks, then with the stones beat the earth with all their strength. And in this maner (as he reported) they continued aboue two houres.

After this ended, they which haue wiues take them apart, and withdraw themselues seuerally into the wood all night. The next morning, asoone as they saw the Sunne rise, they pointed to him to come with them to our shippe: and hauing receiued their men from vs, they came with fiue or six of their Canoas and Company houering about our ship, to whom (because it was Sabbath day) I signed they should depart, and at the next Sun rising we would goe along with them to their houses:[54] which they vnderstood (as we thought) and departed, some of their Canoas coursing about the Iland, and the other directly towards the maine.[55]

[54] Once more we get an indication that there was no concept on Rosier's part of the dwellings of the Native people. They were, no doubt, as much at home on the islands, sleeping under the stars, as they were at their summer encampment, which in any case was not their permanent abode.

[55] It is difficult to interpret "coursing about the iland" but here we have the first indication of the presence of Natives from two different places. The word of the ship's presence at Burnt Island had spread along the coast. In all probability the canoes which disappeared around the island indicate some Indians traveling to the west of Allen Island, perhaps those from Muscongus or Pemaquid, who eventually were captured. The others, "directly towards the maine" would have been those from the Pleasant Point peninsula in Cushing.

This day, about fiue a clocke after noone, came three other Canoas from the maine, of which some had beene with vs before;[56] and they came aboord vs, and brought vs Tabacco, which we tooke with them in their pipes, which were made of earth, very strong, blacke, and short, containing a great quantity: some Tabacco they gaue vnto our Captaine, and some to me, in very ciuil kind maner. We requited them with bread and peaze, which they carried to their Company on shore, seeming very thankefull. After supper they returned with their Canoa to fetch vs a shore to take Tabacco with them there; with whom six or seuen of vs went and caried some trifles, if per-aduenture they had any trucke[57], among which I caried some few biskits, to try if they would exchange for them, seeing they so liked to eat them. When we came at shore, they most kindly entertained vs, taking vs by the hands, as they had obserued we did to them aboord, in token of welcome, and brought vs to sit downe by the fire, where sat together thirteene of them. They filled their Tabacco pipe, which was then the

---

[56] Indians arriving "from the maine," some who had been with them before, shows either curiosity or a coy persistence, which caused them to return even though Rosier had indicated that they should return the following morning.

[57] Trucke, from the French word *troquer*, was a term indicating trade or barter. Rosier keeps returning to the necessity to "trucke" when it seems that his Abenaki visitors, being more interested in satisfying their curiosity, came to socialize. The notion that these people would be interested in barter seems to have been something acquired from knowledge of the French experience on the Saint Lawrence. The fact that on board *Archangell* the Englishmen had seemingly endless supplies of combs, looking glasses, knives, and other trinkets would support the idea that, whatever Waymouth's original destination, he intended to test trade of some kind. The Natives of the Maine Coast had yet to become accustomed to visits from Europeans and, although Champlain had had contact and some trade with the Bashebas and his people at Kenduskeag the previous September, these coastal people might have had knowledge of European trade, but probably no firsthand experience.

short claw of a Lobster, which will hold ten of our pipes full, and we dranke of their excellent Tabacco as much as we would with them;[58] but we saw not any great quantity to trucke for; and it seemed they had not much left of old, for they spend a great quantity yeerly by their continuall drinking: and they would signe vnto vs, that it was growen yet but a foot aboue ground, and would be aboue a yard high, with a leafe as broad as both their hands. They often would (by pointing to one part of the maine Eastward) signe vnto vs, that their Bashebas (that is their King) had plenty of furres, and much Tabacco.[59] When we had sufficiently taken Tabacco with them, I shewed some of our trifles for trade; but they made signe that they had there nothing to exchange; for (as I after conceiued) they had beene fishing and fowling, and so came thither to lodge that night by vs: for when we were ready to come away, they shewed vs great cups made very wittily of barke, in forme almost square, full of a red berry about the bignesse of a bullis, which they did eat, and gaue vs by handfuls; of which (though I

[58] English pipes of the time were quite small, but this statement, if not exaggeration, gives an idea of the size of the lobsters being caught along the shore by the Indians. By reference to drinking tobacco he refers to inhaling, as we call it today. Lest one think that the use of tobacco was, in those times of its early discovery and use by the English, desirable, or even acceptable, we should note that King James I opposed it in a letter which he titled *A Counter-Blast to Tobacco* in 1604 (Beer, 1922). In the letter he said that the public use of tobacco was so widespread that many were forced to take up the habit in order not to appear singular. Is there nothing new under the sun?

[59] Although not very explicit, by extension this statement indicates that the Basheba and his people, although their permanent village was at Orono, spent the summer somewhere on Penobscot Bay. Since, as is known from Champlain's narratives (Champlain, *Works*, 1, 1922, p. 283-96), the Basheba was seen near the entrance to Penobscot Bay, he would not have been far away. In fact, the constant entreaties of the Indian visitors to come to the "maine" to trade with the Bashebas would support the idea that they were in regular communication with him and had his sanction, even desire, for such a visit.

liked not the taste) yet I kept some, because I would by no meanes but accept their kindnesse. They shewed me likewise a great piece of fish, whereof I tasted, and it was fat like Porpoise; and another kinde of great scaly fish, broiled on the coales, much like white Salmon, which the Frenchmen call Aloza, for these they would haue bread; which I refused, because in maner of exchange, I would alwayes make the greatest esteeme I could of our commodities whatsoeuer; although they saw aboord our Captaine was liberall to give to the end we might allure them still to frequent vs.[60] Then they shewed me foure yoong goslings, for which they required foure biskets, but I offered them two; which they tooke and were well content.

At our departure they made signe, that if any of vs would stay there on shore, some of them would go lie aboord vs: at which motion two of our Company stayed with them, and three of the Saluages lodged with vs in maner as the night before.

[60] Thinking that the Natives should be interested in trade, he made a rather obvious attempt to convince them that this was his purpose as well, not to mention that he could drive a hard bargain! As we have seen, they appear not to have been much interested in trade. However, to satisfy what they thought was the Englishman's interest, they appealed to him to go to the Basheba. Waymouth's and Rosier's reticence to do that after all the talk about trade surely must have made them suspicious.

The overt nature of his need to "allure them still to frequent us," presumably for the further study of their language and habits, seems to signify that there was already a resolve to capture some of the visitors when the opportunity presented itself.

Early the next morning, being Munday the third of Iune, when they had brought our men aboord, they came about our ship, earnestly by signes desiring that we would go with them along to the maine, for that there they had Furres and Tabacco to traffique with vs.[61] Wherefore our Captaine manned the light-horseman with as many men as he could well, which were about fifteene with rowers and all; and we went along with them. Two of their canoas they sent away before, and they which lay aboord vs all night, kept company with vs to direct vs.

This we noted as we went along, they in their Canoa with three oares, would at their will go ahead of vs and about vs, when we rowed with eight oares strong; such was their swiftnesse, by reason of the lightnesse and artificiall composition of their Canoa and oares.

When we came neere the point we saw their fires,[62] where they intended to land, and where they imagined some few of vs would come on shore with our merchandize, as we had accus-

[61] The persistence of this particular group of Natives can leave no doubt that their evening visit was preplanned in spite of Rosier's belief that they had returned for "fishing and fowling." The mainland visit had been promised and they were making sure it would happen. Whether the reason was an innocent attempt to introduce Captain Waymouth and his men to the villagers, or more sinister, can only be surmised. It seems obvious, however, that if they had goods available for trade they could as easily have carried them to the ship as have Waymouth come to the mainland. There is beginning to be the appearance of "cat and mouse," but who is the cat and who is the mouse is still not clear.

[62] As we have stated, the point referred to here is the southern tip of the Pleasant Point peninsula in Cushing, Maine. By way of explanation: In 1612 William Strachey, in his *Historie of travaile into virginia Britania* gave Robert Davies's account of the arrival of the Popham Colony to this coast, in which he described sighting "the land called Segohquet." In 1615 Captain John Smith also made mention of "Segocket" as being a place sequentially between Mecadacut (presentday Camden) and Nus-concus (presentday Muscongus or Bremen). What these English scribes heard, phonetically, that caused them to write "Segohquet" and "Sego-cket" was a placename constituting the root *Segou*, meaning it breaks, or

tomed before; when they had often numbered our men very diligently, they scoured away to their Campany, not boubting we
would haue followed them. But when we perceiued this, and knew

is broken, with -*keag*, signifying a "point" such as a protrusion of land
into a river, or a point of land between the confluence of two rivers, or a
main river and a branch river. In this case we construe the term as meaning "the broken-point place" (Aubery dictionary, 1995).

The specific location of "Segocket," as a place, and even whether it
was a large area, a point of land, or part of a river, has eluded historians
for nearly four hundred years, but a relatively recent archeological discovery has shed new light on the matter. In 1980 the St. George Archeological Survey was initiated. It was conducted by Stuart A. Eldridge, as
part fulfillment of the dissertation requirements for his Ph.D. in Anthro-
pology at the University of Pennsylvania. The project, under the auspices of the Maine Historic Preservation Commission, included a shell
midden, which was named the Sparkes site, for its modern landowners
(Maine Archeological Survey site location 17-6). The Sparkes site is
located just east of the tip of the point at the western end of Pleasant
Point Gut in Cushing, Maine. The site seems to cover an area of aprox-
imately 400 square meters. The survey was consided preliminary and
only three test pits, one by two meters in size, were dug. Although house
floors were not encountered, the area included would certainly indicate
a seasonal occupation, with all its attendant activity. Many artifacts were
taken, including some of English colonial origin, most of which indicate
a late ceramic/early contact period occupation.

As can be seen from this evidence, there was a place of Indian occupation, probably a summer encampment, located on Pleasant Point ("the
broken-point place" or perhaps just "broken point") just across the gut
from Gay Island, sometime during the period under our present consideration. If one considers that Gay Island is only an island by the nature
of the tiny gut running between it and Pleasant Point, one might say the
point and the island are "broken" by the gut. It is the opinion of this
writer that this place was, in fact, John Smith's "Segocket" and, with further evidence, as we shall see, the place of Owen Griffin's encounter
with the Natives.

not either their intents, or number of Saluages on the shore, our Captaine, after consultation, stood off, and wefted them to vs, determining that I should go on shore first to take a view of them, and what they had to traffique: if he, whom at our first sight of them seemed to be of most respect among them, and being then in the Canoa, would stay as a pawne for me. When they came to vs (notwithstanding all our former courtesies) he vtterly refused, but would leave a young Saluage; and for him our Captaine sent Griffin in their Canoa, while we lay hulling a little off.[63] Griffen at his returne reported, they had there assembled together, as he numbered them, two hundred eighty three Saluages,[64] [with] every one his bowe and arrowes, with their dogges, and wolves which they keep tame at their command, and not any thing to ex-

[63] Rosier indicates that once Griffin went ashore to survey the situation, Waymouth took his Light Horseman "a little off" to wait for Griffin's report. Waymouth's waiting took place near the end of Davis Point approximately three-quarters of a mile across Davis Cove from the village at the end of Pleasant Point. This is evidenced by the fact that while waiting on the shore of Davis Point, Waymouth's boatswain, Thomas King, whiled away the time by pecking an inscription bearing his name, Thos. King, with a cross and the date 1605, in the bedrock on the shore. In 1978 the inscription, which had been known by a few residents for generations, was authenticated by the Maine Historic Preservation Commission, and placed on the National Register of Historic Places.

[64] Whether there was mistrust on both sides is difficult to determine, but certainly there was mistrust on Waymouth's part. He was obviously wary of some trap from the beginning of this venture. It is probable that without the interpreting skills of James Rosier (such as they were) on shore to pave the way for some kind of understanding of the situation, the moment was lost. As to the danger presented, it is difficult to believe that fifteen men confined to a comparatively slow-moving, open boat, regardless of how well armed, would have had a chance to say a prayer if these people really had malice in mind.

A Rubbing of Thomas King's Inscription

change at all; but would haue drawen vs further vp into a little narrow nooke of a riuer,[65] for their furres, as they pretended.

These things considered, we began to ioyne them in the ranke of other Saluages, who haue been by trauellers in most discoueries found very treacherous: neuer attempting mischiefe, vntill by some remisnesse, fit opportunity afoordeth them certaine ability to execute the same. Wherefore after good auice taken, we determined so soone as we could to take some of them, least (being suspitious we had discouered their plots) they should absent themselues from vs.[66]

Tuesday, the fourth of June, our men tooke Cod and Haddocke with hooks by our ship side, and Lobsters very great:[67] which before we had not tried.

About eight a clocke this day we went on shore with our boats, to fetch aboord water and wood, our Captaine leauing

[65] Knowing now where this encounter took place allows us to know what Griffin perceived as "a little narrow nooke of a river." Many other places in the vicinity might fit the description, but none could fit it more perfectly than Pleasant Point Gut. Very narrow and tidal, when viewed from the vantage point of the Native village site, it appears to be a tiny river. Here is another of the ironies of the Waymouth adventure. What Griffin could not see was that if he were to travel along this "little narrow nooke of a river" for about one mile to its eastern end, he would have discovered the St. George River; and up the St. George two miles from the east end of the gut he might have seen the main village at *Penapske-ot* where these "two hundred eighty three Salvages" lived during the winter months. There he might even have seen the furs which they had proffered.

Full knowledge of this encounter and its circumstances is the evidence on which we form the belief that Waymouth did not know that the St. George River existed. If he had been there the confusion over the "little nook of a river," and where it led, would not have existed.

[66] At last James Rosier says what has obviously been on his mind for some time. However, only after he has made his rather thinly disguised and hypocritical rationale.

[67] This business of catching large lobsters with a hook and line is incredible. This can only be an editorial error or a description of two unconnected events in the same sentence.

word with the Gunner in the shippe, by discharging a musket, to giue notice if they espied any Canoa comming: which they did about ten a clocke. He therefore being carefull they should be kindly entreated, requested me to go aboord, intending with dispatch to make what haste after he could.[68] When I came to the ship, there were two Canoas, and in either of them three Saluages; of whom two were below at the fire, the other staied in their Canoas about the ship; and because we could not entice them abord, we gaue them a cann of pease and bread, which they carried to the shore to eat. But one of them brought backe our canne presently and staid abord with the other two; for he being yoong, of a ready capacity, and one we most desired to bring with vs into England, had receiued exceeding kinde vsage at our hands, and was therefore much delighted in our company.[69] When our Captaine was come, we consulted how to catch the other three at shore, which we performed thus. We manned the light horseman with 7 or 8 men, one standing before carried our box of marchandise, as we were woont when I went to traffique with them, and a platter of pease, which meat they loued: but before we were landed, one of them (being too suspitiously fearefull of his own good) withdrew himselfe into the wood. The other two met vs on the shore side, to receiue the pease, with whom we went vp the cliffe to their fire and sate downe with them,[70] and whiles we were discussing how to catch the third man who was gone, I opened the box, and

[68] It can be seen here that Captain Waymouth is setting the trap of a well-orchestrated plan to take the next small group of Natives to arrive. At the same time he is taking the prudent step of topping off his supply of wood and water, in the eventuality that he should have to hurriedly leave the land.

[69] Rosier would seem to be saying here that they may have already picked some of the Natives that they hoped would be available for the taking. There is no way to identify which of the five he refers to.

[70] "We went up the cliffe to their fire" is further indication that the fire which had been used by the Natives was located on the high northeast point of Allen Island.

shewed them trifles to exchange, thinking thereby to haue banisht feare from the other, and drawen him to returne: but when we could not, we vsed little delay, but svddenly laid hands vpon them. And it was as much as fiue or sixe of vs could doe to get them into the light horseman. For they were strong and so naked as our best hold was by their long haire on their heads: and we would haue beene very loath to haue done them any hurt, which of necessity we had beene constrained to haue done if we had attempted them in a multitude, which we must and would, rather than haue wanted them, being a matter of great importance for the full accomplement of our voyage.[71]

Thus we shipped fiue Saluages, two Canoas, with all their bowes and arrowes.

The next day we made an end of getting our wood aboord, and filled our empty caske with water.

Thursday, the 6 of Iune, we spent in bestowing the canoas upon the orlop safe from hurt, because they were subiect to breaking, which our Captaine was carefull to preuent. Saturday, the eight of Iune (our Captaine being desirous to finish all businesse about this harbour) very early in the morning, with the light horseman, coasted fiue or sixe leagues about the ilands adioining, and sounded all along wheresoeuer we went. He likewise diligently searched the mouth of the harbour, and about the rocks which shew themselues at all times, and are an excellent breach of the water, so as no sea can come in to offend the Harbour. This he did to instruct himselfe, and thereby [be] able to direct others that shall happen to come to this place. For euery where both neere the rocks & in all soundings about the Ilands we neuer

---

[71] Rosier here seems to say that they wished not to harm any of their captives, but they would if it were necessary, since it was a matter of great importance to the accomplishment of the voyage. Perhaps it is stretching a point to note the implication that this was part of the plan for the voyage from its inception in England. Certainly it shows the cold, arrogant side of English colonialism which eventually decimated the population of Native Americans, an attitude which the French were able to exploit for the purpose of turning the Indians against British settlement.

found lesse water than foure and fiue fathoms, which was seldome; but seuen, eight, nine and ten fathoms is continuall by the shore. In some places much deeper vpon clay oaze or soft sand: so that if any bound for this place, should be either driuen or scanted with windes, he shall be able (with his directions) to recouer safely his harbour most securely in water enough by foure severall passages, more then which I thinke no man of iudgement will desire as necessarie.[72]

Vpon one of the Ilands (because it had a pleasant sandy coue for small barks to ride in) we landed, and found hard by the shore a pond of fresh water, which flowed ouer the banks, some what ouergrowen with little shrub trees, and searching vp in the Iland, we saw it fed with a strong run, which with small labour, and little time, might be made to driue a mill. In this Iland, as in the other, were spruce trees of excellent timber and height, able to mast ships of great burthen.[73]

---

[72] This is a very accurate description of the conditions to be found in the vicinity of the Georges Islands. There can be no doubt that the "rocks which shew themselves at all times" at the mouth of the harbor are the Dry Ledges between Allen and Burnt Islands, the "mouth of the harbour" being one of the "four severall passages." Rosier is correct that no sea can come in to offend the harbor, at least from the south. It should be noted, however, that in a southwest breeze the wind funnels between the two islands, increasing its velocity considerably. Anyone who has taken the afternoon ferry from Monhegan to Port Clyde can attest to it. The four entrances would be the aforementioned channel between Burnt Island and Allen Island on the south, the little strait between Allen Island and Benner Island on the west, the area between Davis Island and the Shag Ledges on the north, and the deep area between Burnt Island and Carey Rock or the Shag Ledges on the east.

[73] There is only one possible location for this "pleasant sandy coue with a pond of fresh water hard by the shore" and the description fits perfectly. It is located on the east side of Allen Island adjacent to the Dry Ledges. The pond is now somewhat filled in with eroded topsoil from higher up in the island, but it is obvious and the brook still runs heavily in the spring. Some of the old-growth trees on Allen Island are enormous, even today, and it is doubtful that the trees on the southern half of the island have ever been harvested by man.

While we thus sounded from one place to another in so good deepes, our Captaine to make some triall of the fishing himselfe, caused a hooke or two to be cast out at the mouth of the harbour, not aboue halfe a league from our ship, where in small time only, with the baits which they cut from the fish and three hooks, we got fish enough for our whole Company (though now augmented) for three daies. Which I omit not to report, because it sheweth how great a profit the fishing would be, they being so plentifull, so great and so good, with such conuenient drying as can be wished, neere at hand vpon the rockes.[74]

This day, about one a clocke after noone, came from the Eastward two Canos abord vs, wherein was he that refused to stay with vs for a pawn, and with him sixe other Saluages which we had not seene before, who had beautified themselues after their manner very gallantly, though their clothing was not differing from the former, yet they had newly painted their faces very deep, some all blacke, some red, with stripes of excellent blew ouer their vpper lips, nose and chin. One of them ware a kinde of coronet about his head, made very cunningly, of a substance like stiffe haire coloured red, broad, and more then a handfull in depth, which we imagined to be some ensigne of his superioritie: for he so much esteemed it as he would not for anything exchange the same. Other ware the white feathered skins of some fowle, round about their head, iewels in their eares, and bracelets of little white round

[74] One can only imagine this kind of fishing today, but history has shown that Rosier was not exaggerating. A tremendous industry, based on these stocks of fish, began shortly after Waymouth's visit and continued until a few years ago. Overfishing, which no one thought possible, has depleted the stocks quickly in recent years, and fishing as a way of life is being relegated to history.

bone, fastened together vpon a leather string. These they made
not any shew that they had notice of the other before taken, but
we vnderstood them by their speech and signes, that they came
sent from the Bashebes, and that his desire was that we would
bring vp our ship (which they call as their owne boats, a Quiden)
to his house, being, as they pointed, upon the main towards the
East, from whence they came, and that he would exchange with vs
for Furres and Tabacco.[75] But because our company was but
small, and now our desire was with speed to discouer vp the riuer,
we let them vnderstand, that if their Bashebes would come to vs,
he should be welcome, but we would not remoue to him. Which
when they vnderstood (receiuing of vs bread and fish, and euery of
them a knife) they departed; for we had then no will to stay them

[75] From the time of their aborted attempt at trade on the mainland
on Monday, till one o'clock on Saturday, Rosier has made no mention of
a visit by the people from the mainland. Much is left to conjecture here,
but it would seem that the local Natives must have become as disap-
pointed by Waymouth's refusal to come ashore at Pleasant Point as
Waymouth had been suspicious of their large number, and somehow
this is manifested in a refusal to visit the ship. With this visit, "he that
refused to stay with us as a pawn," who was the leader of the group at
Pleasant Point, arrives. Apparently, in his disappointment over the break
in relations, he has gone to get those with more goods, and the power
to trade them. This visit appears to be of an official nature with a sagamore carrying the invitation to trade once again, only this time as a
direct representative of the Basheba. As we know, Champlain had gone
up the Penobscot in the previous September, and had had friendly trade
with the Basheba, certainly establishing a precedent for this behavior.

We know, as a matter of history, that the six who had arrived on Tuesday were from a village at the Muscongus/Pemaquid peninsula. It is
questionable at this point whether these people from Pleasant Point, or
the representatives of the Basheba from the eastward, are aware of the
capture of the five. Although it may have been a thinly disguised effort
to discover the captives, somehow, it seems that there would have been
more canoe activity around the harbor if an alarm had been raised.
There is no indication at all of the lone survivor on Allen Island.

long abord, least they should discouer the other Saluages which we had stowed below.[76]

Tuesday, the 11 of Iune, we passed vp into the riuer with our ship, about six and twenty miles. Of which I had rather not write, then by my relation to detract from the worthiness thereof. For the river, besides that it is subiect by shipping to bring all traffiques of marchandise, a benefit alwaies accounted the richest treasury to any land: for which cause our Thames hath that due denomination, and France by her nauigable riuers receiueth hir greatest wealth; yet this place of it selfe from God and nature afoordeth as much diuersitie of good commodities, as any reasonable man can wish, for present habitation and planting.[77]

The first and chiefest thing required, is a bold coast and faire land to fall with; the next, a safe harbour for ships to ride in.

---

[76] Once again the efforts of the Basheba are rebuffed by Captain Waymouth and Rosier. This may have been prudent, considering their fear of discovery. However, they are oblivious to the effect that this behavior might have on future voyages. There is a certain arrogance to their approach to the obvious leader of these people and his envoys which characterized most of the English dealings with the Natives. The French, albeit with the same European outlook, took a completely different approach.

The fact that these seven Natives were aboard the ship without seeing or hearing any sign of the others below is another indication that *Archangell* was a good-sized vessel, having more than one deck below the main.

[77] A distance of twenty-six miles from the northeast point of Burnt Island would have taken *Archangell* up the west entrance to Penobscot Bay, either through the Mussel Ridge Channel or outside of Two Bush Island and Monroe Island, to a spot somewhere near Deadman or Beauchamp Point at Rockport. From this location the Camden Hills are all very nearly four and a half miles distant. It is at this point in traveling up the bay that one can see the narrowing ahead caused by the passage between Islesboro and Northport. It is also this area, between Rockland Harbor and Camden that Waymouth and Rosier considered the entrance to the "river itself." Significantly, it is also at this point in his journal that Rosier makes his first reference to "habitation and planting."

The first is a speciall attribute to this shore, being most free from sands or dangerous rocks in a continuall depth, with a most excellent land-fall, which is the first Iland we fell with, named by vs, Saint Georges Iland.[78] For the second, by iudgement of our Captaine, who knoweth most of the coast of England, and most of other countries, (hauing beene experienced by imployments in discoueries and travels from his childhood) and by opinion of others of good iudgement in our shippe, heere are more good harbours for ships of all burthens, than England can affoord, and far more secure from all winds and weathers, than any in England, Scotland, France or Spain. For besides, without the riuer in the channel and sounds about the ilands adioining to the mouth thereof, no better riding can be desired for an infinite number of ships.[79] The riuer it selfe as it runneth vp into the main very nigh forty miles toward the great mountaines, beareth in bredth a mile, sometimes three quarters, and halfe a mile is the narrowest, where you shall neuer haue vnder 4 and 5 fathoms water hard by the shore, but 6,7,8,9, and 10 fathoms all along, and on both sides euery halfe mile very gallant Coues, some able to conteine almost a hundred saile, where the ground is excellent soft oaze with a

[78] Sand bottom is rare on the Maine Coast, as their sounding lead accurately detected. Nearly the whole Maine Coast has been referred to by marriners as a rockpile. But to give Rosier credit, most deep rivers and channels which are obvious as such to the eye are amazingly free of hidden obstacles. Monhegan has been, since the time of this narrative, the primary landfall for vessels coming in from sea bound up the Penobscot.

[79] If one takes a careful look at a chart of Penobscot Bay and its approaches, or views it from a boat, it quickly becomes obvious that there is much less exaggeration in Rosier's statement than the exclamatory nature of the narrative would indicate. Perhaps Rockland Harbor is the best example, and what Rosier had in mind. In this case "without the river" refers to anything below Rockport.

tough clay vnder for anker hold, and where ships may ly without either cable or anker, only mored to the shore with a hauser.[80]

It floweth by their iudgement eighteen or twenty foot at high water.[81]

Heere are made by nature most excellent places, as docks to graue or Carine ships of all burthens: secured from all windes, which is such a necessary incomparable benefit, that in few places in England, or in any parts of Christendome, art, with great charges, can make the like.[82]

---

[80] Here the reference to forty miles might be somewhat confusing. At first thought this forty miles seems to be the same as that described when Captain Waymouth returned from his initial survey of the river. Sears Island is forty miles from the anchorage at Burnt Island and is no doubt where he turned around during that initial survey, seeing that the river narrowed considerably at Fort Point and not wishing to be exposed without flank armor. However, here Rosier speaks of "the river itself" and this forty miles refers to the part of the Penobscot beginning at Jameson or Deadman Point in Rockport to the farthest point which was explored at Brewer.

This statement is absolutely without exaggeration when applied to the river from Rockport to Brewer. The gallant coves are certainly Camden Harbor, Ducktrap Harbor, Belfast Bay, and Searsport Harbor, all on the west shore, with Gilkey Harbor and Seal Harbor on Islesboro, and Bucksport and Marsh Bay farther up.

As for mooring to the shore with a hawser, it may be worth noting that there are places in the area of Northport that an aircraft carrier could, with proper fendering, actually accomplish this, as the water is over one hundred feet deep within thirty feet of the shore.

[81] Here is an exaggeration, if we are looking for one. The spring tide range at Camden is closer to eleven feet.

[82] Clipper ships were built in Rockland, and families became wealthy from the building and repair of ships in Penobscot Bay towns such as Belfast and Searsport in the nineteenth century, attesting to the foresight in this remark.

Besides the bordering land is a most rich neighbor trending all along both sides, in an equall plaine, neither mountainous nor rocky, but verged with a greene bordure of grasse, both make tender vnto the beholder of hir pleasant fertility, if by clensing away the woods she were converted to meddow.

The wood she beareth is not shrubbish fit only for fewell, but goodly tall Firre, Spruce, Birch, Beech, Oke, which in many places is not so thicke, but may with small labour be made feeding ground, being plentifull like the outward Ilands with fresh water, which streameth downe in many places.

As we passed with a gentle winde vp with our ship in this riuer, any man may conceiue with what admiration we all consented in ioy. Many of our Company who had beene trauellers in sundry countries, and in the most famous riuers, yet affirmed them not comparable to this they now beheld. Some that were with Sir Walter Ralegh in his voyage to Guiana, in the discouery of the riuer Oranoque, which echoed fame to the worlds eares, gaue reasons why it was not to be compared with this, which wanteth the dangers of many shoules, and broken ground, wherewith that was incombred. Others before that notable riuer in the West Indies called Rio Grande; some before the riuer of Loyer, the riuer Seine, and of Burdeaux in France; which although they be great and goodly riuers, yet it is no detraction from them to be accounted inferior to this, which not only yeeldeth all the foresaid pleasant profits, but also appeared infallibly to vs free from all inconueniences.

I will not prefer it before our riuer Thames, because it is Englands richest treasure; but we all did wish those excellent Harbours, good deeps in a continuall conuenient breadth, and small tide gates, to be aswell therein for our countries good, as we found them here (beyond our hopes) in certaine, for those to whom it shall please God to grant this land for habitation; which if it had, with the other inseparable adherent commodities here to be found; then I would boldly affirme it to be the most rich, beautiful, large & secure harbouring riuer that the world affoordeth.[83]

Wednesday, the twelfth of Iune, our Captaine manned his light horseman with 17 men, and ranne vp from the ship riding in the riuer vp to the codde thereof,[84] where we landed, leauing six to keepe the light-horseman till our returne. Ten of vs with our shot, and some armed, with a boy to carry powder and match, marched vp into the countrey towardes the mountaines, which we descried at our first falling with the land. Vnto some of them the riuer brought vs so neere, as we iudged our selues when we landed

[83] These remarks seem to be partly real-estate promotion and partly genuine awe. Both are to be understood. He certainly had to satisfy the backers of the voyage with something to justify the expense that they had incurred. As to the awe, the psychological effects of the discovery of a nearly uninhabited, tranquil new land must have been strong indeed. Once again we should remember that Rosier's notes were written while he was seeing the Maine Coast at its very best, and in truth he is not the only writer who has expressed these sentiments.

[84] Rosier seems to have thought of west Penobscot Bay—the large, open area bounded by Rockland, Owls Head, Vinalhaven, North Haven, and Rockport—as the "codde." This is consistent with usage of the word at the time as meaning a sack, a bag, or vulgarly, as a scrotum (often a certain item of male attire was called a "codpiece"). Here, Rosier seems to use the term to indicate the entire bay, including Rockland Harbor. Here they travel in the shallop up to the upper side of the codde, where there was a narrowing just above the ship at anchor, probably between Mark Island and Ogier Point.

to have beene within a league of them:[85] but we marched vp about foure miles in the maine, and passed ouer three hills:[86] and because the weather was parching hot, and our men in their armour not able to travel farre and returne that night to our ship, we resolued not to passe any further, being all very weary of so tedious and laboursome a travell.

On this march we passed ouer very good ground, pleasant and fertile, fit for pasture, for the space of some three miles, hauing but little wood, and that Oke like stands left in our pastures in

[85] From this area, the Camden Hills look to be about three miles away, as Rosier suggests. There can be no doubt that these are the mountains described, and that the Ogier Point area is the location of this event. The east side of Megunticook Mountain literally starts at the river's edge above Camden and its five sister mountains (Bald, Ragged, Spruce, Pleasant, and Meadow) form a continuous line to the southwest of it. Waymouth had viewed these mountains from this vantage point, while passing on his earlier survey of the river, on 10 June. He had apparently resolved to climb one in an attempt to get some idea of the extent and nature of the country he had discovered.

Admittedly, the Mount Battie area was much closer to the river, therefore more accessible. There would have been an additional dimension to his interest in this specific place on the river, however. While first exploring the river, Waymouth would have noticed that the Rockport/Camden area, at the riverside, had hardwoods, rather than the spruce forest which exists along most of the shoreline of the lower river. The fertile nature of the soil was indicated by this area of somewhat level ground containing deciduous forest. As he viewed it from the shore, looking inland at this point, he must certainly have been thinking about a possible future habitation location.

[86] From Ogier Point their travel in a straight northwesterly direction toward Ragged Mountain would have taken them over three low hills in about three miles, as measured in a straight line, not accounting for the additional distance caused by the terrain.

England, good and great fit timber for any vse.[87] Some small Birch, Hazle and Brake, which might in small time with few men be cleansed and made good arable land: but as it now is will feed cattle of all kindes with fodder enough for summer and winter. The soile is blacke, bearing sundry hearbs, grasse, and strawberries bigger than ours in England. In many places are lowe Thickes like our Copisses of small yoong wood. And surely it did resemble a stately parke, wherein appeare some old trees with high withered tops, and other flourishing with liuing greene boughs. Vpon the hills grow notable high timber trees, masts for ships of 400 tun: and at the bottome of euery hill, a little run of fresh water: but the furthest and last we passed, ran with a great streame able to driue a mill.[88]

We might see in some places where fallow Deere and Hares had beene, and by the rooting of ground we supposed wilde hogs had ranged there, but we could descrie no beast, because our noise still chased them from vs.

We were no sooner come aboord our light-horseman, returning towards our ship, but we espied a Canoa comming from

[87] Their route probably took them from the shore up over, or very close by, what is now part of the pasture of a well-known cattle-breeding farm named by its present owners, Aldemere Farm. Going back to the eighteenth century it was known as the Ogier Farm. Although the landscape has no doubt changed considerably, the description of the area fits remarkably well. The hardwoods still predominate where wild growth continues to exist. The terrain and soil are certainly adequate, for the Goose River Golf Course has been built on what then would have been the east side of the third hill. His enthusiasm for the benefits of this location for cultivation perfectly expresses the reason for the voyage.

[88] When they finally decided they had gone far enough, they had reached the Goose River, about one mile from the base of Ragged Mountain, as the crow flies. The Goose River is a tiny, swift-running river (some would say brook) which drains the watershed between Bald and Ragged Mountains into Rockport Harbor. Here, we should mention that the Goose River had a mill on it long ago, at Simonton's Corner.

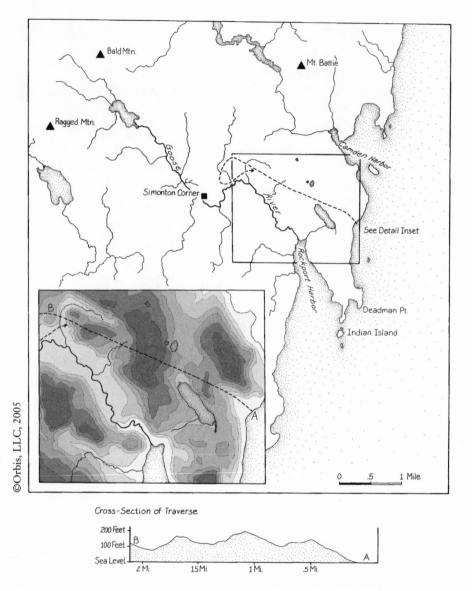

Bald Mtn.

Mt. Battie

Ragged Mtn.

Goose River

Simonton Corner

Camden Harbor

See Detail Inset

Rockport Harbor

Deadman Pt.

Indian Island

B

A

0   .5   1 Mile

Cross-Section of Traverse

200 Feet
100 Feet
Sea Level

B

A

2 Mi.   1.5 Mi.   1 Mi.   .5 Mi.

The March into the Country

the further part of the Cod of the riuer Eastward, which hasted to vs;[89] wherein with two others, was he who refused to stay for a pawne: and his comming was very earnestly importing to haue one of our men to go lie on the shore with their Bashebes (who was there on shore, as they signed) and then the next morning he would come to our ship with many Furres and Tabacco. This we perceiued to be only a meere deuice to get possesion of any of our men, to ransome all thos which we had taken, which their naturall policy could not so shadow, but we did easily discouer and prevent. These meanes were by this Saluage practised, because we had one of his kinsemen prisoner, as we iudged by his most kinde vsage of him being aboord vs together.[90]

[89] Here Rosier uses the term *cod* again (albeit with different spelling). This time, however, he says, "from the further part of the cod of the river eastward." This we interpret to be on the opposite side of the cod, coming from the vicinity of perhaps North Haven, Deer Isle, or even the Castine area. This fits with previous events as we see that this is the same messenger as was sent from the Basheba previously at Pentecost Harbor. Their passage up the Penobscot toward the homeland of the Basheba must certainly have caused the concern of these people. They have obviously been aware of *Archangell*'s movements and appear to Rosier coming from the eastward.

[90] Rosier here seems to say that the messenger has communicated that because they have treated the Natives on board so well, he would like some member of the ship's company to come back to receive the hospitality of the Basheba till the next day, when they could trade. If Rosier's understanding was correct, this was the first concrete evidence that the local people were aware of the situation of their countrymen. To get them back alive must have been of great concern. Captain Waymouth's refusal to send a hostage is, at this point, certainly understandable.

At this point there appears to be an omission from the narrative of a movement of *Archangell*. We have no doubt that in the afternoon or early evening, after returning from the overland trek and having the encounter just described, Captain Waymouth sailed his ship up to Fort Point, at Stockton Springs. This would probably not have required more than four or five hours with a following wind. The omission cannot be accounted for, but *Archangell* was certainly at Fort Point at 2 A.M. the following morning.

Thursday, the 13 of Iune, by two a clocke in the morning (because our Captaine would take the helpe and aduantage of the tide) in the light-horseman with our Company well provided and furnished with armour and shot both to deffend and offend; we went from the ship vp to that part of the riuer which trended Westward into the maine, to search that: and we carried with vs a Crosse, to erect at that point, (which because it was not daylight, we left on the shore vntill our returne backe;[91] when we set it vp in maner as the former. For this (by the way) we diligently ob-serued, that in no place, either about the Ilands, or vp in the maine, or alongst the riuer, we could dicerne any token or signe, that euer any Christian had beene before; of which either by cut-ting wood, digging for water, or seting vp crosses (a thing neuer ommitted by any Christian trauellers) we should haue perceiued some mention left.[92]

But to returne to our riuer, further vp into which we then rowed by estimation twenty miles, the beauty and goodnesse whereof I can not by relation sufficiently demonstrate. That which I can say in general is this; What profit or pleasure soeuer is de-scribed and truly veruified in the former part of the riuer, is wholly doubled in this; for the bredth and depth is such, that any

[91] Rosier's statement that they "went from the ship to that part of the river which trended westward into the maine" is obvious. The river does, in fact, trend westward at Bucksport, and they would have been there before daylight as Rosier stated. They would have placed the cross upon the point that is now Fort Knox, a place that can be seen by any vessel ascending the river. The point can also be seen clearly from the Bucksport suspension bridge.

[92] Based on the narrative of Samuel de Champlain, it is not true that no other Christian had been there before. Champlain had ascended the river in September of 1604 and traded with the Basheba. Champlain traveled westward, along the coast again, in July of 1605 and it is remark-able that Captain Waymouth and Captain Champlain did not meet then.

ship drawing 17 or 18 foot water might have passed as farre as we went with our light-horseman,[93] and by all our mens iudgement much further, because we left it in so good depth and bredth; which is so much the more to be esteemed of greater woorth, by how much it trendeth further vp into the maine: for from the place of our ships riding in the harbour at the entrance into the sound, to the furthest part we were in this riuer, by our estimation was not much less than threescore miles.[94]

From each banke of this riuer are diuers branching streames into the maine, whereby is affoorded an vnspeakable profit by the conueniency of transportation from place to place, which in some countries is both chargeable, and not so fit, by cariages on waine, or horsebacke.[95]

[93] Twenty miles would have gotten them to the Waterworks Falls (so-called) just above the confluence of the Kenduskeag Stream with the Penobscot. It is doubtful, however, that they got quite that far as they would most certainly have seen the Waterworks Falls and mentioned them. They probably reached some point between Sedgeunkedunk Stream at South Brewer and where the new highway bridge passes over the river today. The depth of water there would have been 20 feet at low water, confirming Rosier's statement. (Chart No. 13309, Penobscot River, NOAA, National Ocean Service, 24th ed., 1988.)

[94] Using a distance of twenty miles from Fort Point at Stockton Springs to the extremity of travel up the river, means that they travelled about sixty miles from the anchorage at Burnt Island to that point. The "three score miles" were, no doubt, based on noon latitude positions taken at the Dry Ledges and at Brewer, or wherever he was on the river, at noon on Thursday, the thirteenth of June by his Julian calendar. Considering the fact that he had no horizon in the river, his estimate seems very good.

[95] There are, as Rosier states, diverse branching streams into the Penobscot River, and although one might today tend to discount their value to commerce, it should be noted that thousands of tons of granite were shipped out of the Marsh River at Frankfort during the nineteenth century.

[81]

Heere we saw great store of fish, some great, leaping above water, which we iudged to be Salmons.[96] All along is an excellent mould of ground. The wood in most places, especially on the east side,very thinne, chiefly oke and some small yoong birch, bordering low vpon the riuer; all fit for medow and pasture ground: and in that space we went, we had on both sides the riuer many plaine plots of medow, some three or foure acres, some of eight or nine: so as we iudged in the whole to be between thirty and forty acres of good grasse, and where the armes run out into the maine, there likewise went a space on both sides of cleere grasse, how far we know not, in many places we might see paths made to come down to the watering.

The excellencie of this part of the riuer, for his good breadth, depth, and fertile bordering ground, did so rauish vs all with variety of pleasantnesse, as we could not tell what to commend, but only admired; some compared it to the riuer Seuerne, (but in a higher degree) and we all concluded (as I verily thinke we might rightly) that we should neuer see the like riuer in euery degree equall, vntill it pleased God we beheld the same againe. For the farther we went, the more pleasing it was to euery man, alluring vs still with expectation of better, so as our men, although they had with great labour rowed long and eat nothing (for we carried with vs no victuall, but a little cheese and bread) yet they were so refreshed with the pleasant beholding thereof, and so loath to forsake it, as some of them affirmed, they would have continued willingly with that only fare and labour 2 daies; but the tide not

[96] The Penobscot River was once one of the largest spawning places for Atlantic salmon in America. During the nineteenth century their population was decimated by the industrial pollution of the logging industry and prevention of their returning to spawn by hydroelectric-power dams. Today, with industrial pollution reduced considerably and the advent of fish ladders, we are just beginning to see their return to this river.

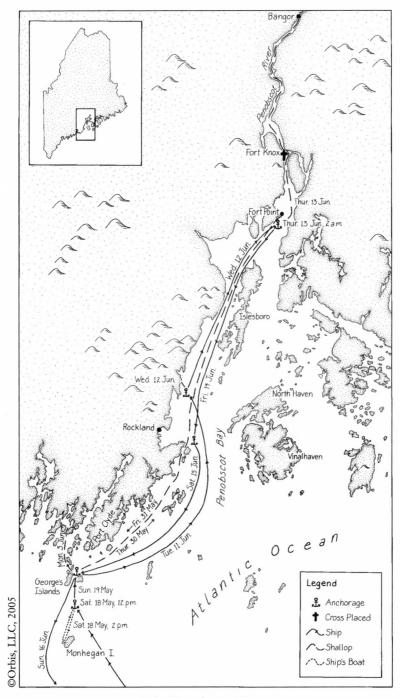

The Penobscot River

[83]

suffering vs to make any longer stay (because we were to come backe with the tide) and our Captaine better knowing what was fit then we, and better what they in labour were able to endure, being verie loath to make any desperate hazard, where so little necessitie required, thought it best to make returne, because whither we had discouered was sufficient to conceiue that the riuer ran very far into the land. For we passed six or seuen miles, altogether fresh water (whereof we all dranke) forced vp by the flowing of the salt:[97] which after a great while eb, where we left it, by breadth of channell and depth of water was likely to run by estimation of our whole company an vnknowen way farther: the search whereof our Captaine hath left till his returne, if it shall so please God to dispose of him and vs.

For we hauing now by the direction of the omnipotent disposer of all good intents (far beyond the period of our hopes) fallen with so bold a coast, found so excellent and secure harbour, for as many ships as any nation professing Christ is able to set forth to sea, discouered a riuer, which the all-creating God, with his most liberall hand, hath made aboue report notable with his foresaid blessings, bordered with a land, whose pleasant fertility bewraieth it selfe to be the garden of nature, wherein she only intended to delight hir selfe, hauing hitherto obscured it to any, except to a purblind generation, whose vnderstanding it hath pleased God so to darken, as they can neither dicerne, vse, or rightly esteeme the vnualuable riches in middest whereof they live sensually content with the barke and outward rinds, as neither knowing

---

[97] To the extremity of their travel up the Penobscot River they were in tidal water. The flow of fresh water out of the river, however, would have been at the surface near the limit of tide, and what they experienced would certainly have been normal in the location that is given.

the sweetnes of the inward marrow, nor acknowledging the Deity of the Almighty giver:[98] Hauing I say thus far proceeded, and hauing some of the inhabitant nation (of best vnderstanding we saw among them) who (learning our language) may be able to giue vs further instruction, concerning all the premised particulars, as also of their gouernours, and gouernment, situation of townes, and what else shall be conuenient which by no means otherwise we could by any obseruation of our selves learne in a long time: our Captaine now wholy intended his prouision for speedy returne. For although the time of yeere and our victuall were not so spent, but we could have made a longer voyage, in searching farther and trading for good commodities, yet as they might haue beene much profitable, so (our company being small) much more preiudiciall to the whole state of our voyage, which we were most regardfull now not to hazard.[99] For we supposing not a little present

[98] This, of course, is Rosier's (Hakluyt, his editor's) reasoning for why this land should be taken from its inhabitants and rightful owners. It has taken nearly four hundred years for people to see the folly in this kind of thinking. Only in very recent years have we seen the real cost of mankind's "knowing the...inward marrow." In truth, America was blessed with all the features which Rosier attributed to it and because his view was limited, far more that he could not have imagined. Today, we can't imagine it either. Not because our view is limited, but because it has mostly been exploited by the voracious appetite of "civilized man." Not even the "purblind generation," who very tentatively coexisted with nature for over ten thousand years, and considered themselves part of it, could stand in the way of such arrogance.

[99] This statement shows the intent, at least Rosier's, of using the captured Indians as a source of information for the backers of future voyages. It pretty accurately describes the information which has eventually come to us as a small (and perhaps incomplete) tract, called *Mawooshen* (Purchas, *Pilgrimes*, IV, 1624; XIX, 1906, p. 400), which indicates the possible connection of Rosier with it, if not its outright authorship.

Once again we are given some idea of the size and ability of *Archangell*. She had been gone from England from the first of April until the thirteenth of June and apparently had enough stores for much more than a month remaining. Of course the bulky firewood and water had been replenished several times, but the space required for storage of dried food goods alone must have been considerable.

priuate profit, but a publique good, and true zeale of promulgating Gods holy Church, by planting Christianity, to be the sole intent of the honourable setters foorth of this discouery; thought it generally most expedient, by our speedy returne, to giue the longer space of time to make provision for so weighty an enterprise.[100]

Friday, the 14 day of Iune, early by foure a clocke in the morning, with the tide, our two boats, and a little help of the winde, we rowed down to the riuers mouth and there came to an anker about eleuen a clocke.[101] Afterward our Captaine in the light horseman searched the sounding all about the mouth and comming to the Riuer, for his certaine instruction of a perfect description.

The next day, being Saturday, we wayed anker, and with a briese from the land, we sailed vp to our watering place, and there stopped, went on shore and filled our empty caske with fresh water.

[100] There appears to be a bit of promotion, self-righteousness, or complete naiveté here, probably some of each. This statement, however, is confirmation that the original intent was a search for a habitable place in America. Here he seems to say that they must hurry back in order that the long process of planning and implementing that enterprise can begin.

[101] The reference here is to the ship's movement from the anchorage at Fort Point "down to the riuers mouth" in the Rockland/Rockport area. Although he states they received "a little help of the winde," there was apparently seven hours of rowing involved. Although the wind and tide must have contributed some to the effort, it seems pulling a ship of *Archangell*'s size would require tremendous effort. Even after anchoring Captain Waymouth continued to explore the lower bay, probably around Rockland, Owls Head, and the Muscle Ridge Islands, requiring more rowing. One can't help but note the amount of rowing which was required on such a voyage, and how little rest some of the crew members must have had between stints.

Our Captaine vpon the rocke in the middest of the harbour obserued the height, latitude, and variation exactly vpon his instruments.

1. Astrolabe.   4. Crosse staffe.
2. Semisphere.   5. And an excellent compasse
3. Ringe instrument.   made for variation.

The certainty whereof, together with the particularities of euery depth and sounding, as well at our falling with the land, as in the discouery, and at our departure from the coast; I refer to his owne relation in the map of his Geographicall description, which for the benefit of others he intendeth most exactly to publish.[102]

The temperature of the climate (albeit a very important matter) I had almost passed without mentioning, because it affoorded to vs no great alteration from our disposition in England; somewhat hotter vp into the maine, because it lieth open to the South, the aire so wholesome, as I suppose not any of vs found our selues at any time more healthfull, more able to labour, nor with better stomacks to such good fare, as we partly brought, and partly found.

---

[102] There is no doubt that Captain Waymouth took more than ordinary pains to identify the specific features of his discovery for the future reference of someone, presumably the captain of the next voyage. In retrospect, this would have amounted to a pilot chart of West Penobscot Bay, something which would have been very useful to future exploitation of that bay by follow-up voyages. It must be kept in mind though, that he had no knowledge of any coastal features except Monhegan, the Georges Islands, the coastline up the west side of Penobscot Bay, and the Camden Hills, all of which lie generally in a north/south line. He had virtually no east/west references along the Maine Coast, limiting what he could impart, except for the details of a major river. In any case, Waymouth probably never did make public his limited knowledge. Others, at the time, had only the information in Rosier's narrative, which, without general knowledge of the area, was obscure, as he apparently intended.

Sunday, the 16 of Iune, the winde being faire, and because we had set out of England vpon a Sunday, made the Ilands vpon a Sunday, and as we doubt not (by Gods appointment) happily fell into our harbour vpon a Sunday; so now (beseeching him still with like prosperity to blesse our returne into England our country, and from thence with his good will and pleasure to hasten our next arriuall there) we waied anker and quit the land vpon a Sunday.

Tuesday, the 18 day, being not run aboue 30 leagues from land, and our Captaine for his certaine knowledge how to fall with the coast, hauing sounded every watch, and from 40 fathoms had come into good deeping, to 70, and so to an hundred: this day the weather being faire, after the foure a clocke watch, when we supposed not to haue found ground so farre from land, and before sounded in above 100 fathoms, we had ground in 24 fathomes.[103] Wherefore our sailes being downe, Thomas King boatswaine,[104] presently cast out a hook, and before he iudged it at ground, was fished and haled vp an exceeding great and well fed Cod: then there were cast out 3 or 4 more, and the fish was so plentiful and so great, as when our Captaine would haue set saile, we all desired him to suffer them to take fish a while, because we were so delighted to see them catch so great fish, so fast as the hooke came downe: some playing with the hooke they tooke by the backe, and one of the mates with two hookes at a lead at fiue draughts together haled vp ten fishes; all were generally very great, some they measured to be fiue foot long, and three foot about.

---

[103] A sailing distance of one hundred and 35 nautical miles in a south, southeast direction would have put *Archangell* in 24 fathoms of water, on the northern edge of Georges Bank. The only possibility short of this would be Cashes Ledge, a distance of sixty nautical miles due south. Even though the distance to Georges Bank is inexplicably greater than described, and Cashes Ledge about the same amount less, Georges seems more likely because, with prevailing southwesterly winds, the course to Cashes would have been too close to the wind for reasonable sailing, especially if going to England.

[104] It should be noted here that this is the only reference to the boatswain, Thomas King, whose name is memorialized in the bedrock on Davis Point, in Cushing.

This caused our Captaine not to maruell at the shoulding, for he perceiued it was a fish banke; which (for our farewell from the land) it pleased God in continuance of his blessings, to give vs knowledge of: the abundant profit whereof should be alone sufficient cause to draw men againe, if there were no other good both in present certaine, and in hope probable to be discouered. To amplify this with words, were to adde light to the sunne: for euery one in the shippe could easily account this present commodity; much more those of iudgement, which knew what belonged to fishing, would warrant (by the helpe of God) in a short voyage with a few good fishers to make a more profitable returne from hence than from New-found-land: the fish being so much greater, better fed and abundant with traine;[105] of which some they desired, and did bring into England to bestow among their friends, and to testifie the true report.

[105] Everything stated here is indisputable as at least fifteen generations of fishermen taking from the abundance of Georges Bank would no doubt attest. There can be no doubt that the fishing industry was the first profitable venture on American shores, probably spurred on by statements in this narrative.

There have been many statements made about the fishermen who must have visited the Gulf of Maine long before Waymouth's time. Presumably this would have produced many contacts between the Natives here and Europeans. This discovery of a previously unknown Georges Bank would appear to refute those claims.

There is no reason to believe that Captain Waymouth's connections to fishing interests in Devonshire had anything to do with remarks here about the abundance of that commodity. Regardless of who the backers were or what their interest was in taking on the voyage, under the circumstances Rosier seems justified in exclaiming about what he observed.

"Traine" was the oil of the cod fish, used at the time for just about everything imaginable, from lubrication to medicine.

After, we kept our course directly for England & with ordinary windes, and sometimes calmes, vpon Sunday the 14 of Iuly about six a clocke at night, we were come into sounding in our channell,[106] but with darke weather and contrary windes, we were constrained to beat vp and down till Tuesday the 16 of Iuly, when by fiue a clocke in the morning we made Sylly; from whence, hindered with calmes and small winds, vpon Thursday the 18 of Iuly about foure a clocke after noone, we came into Dartmouth: which hauen happily (with Gods gracious assistance) we made our last and first Harbour in England.

Further, I haue thought fit here to adde some things worthy to be regarded, which we haue obserued from the Saluages since we tooke them.

First, although at the time when we surprised them, they made their best resistance, not knowing our purpose, nor what we were, nor how we meant to vse them; yet after perceiuing by their kind vsage we intended them no harm, they haue neuer since seemed discontented with vs, but uery tractable, louing, & willing by their best meanes to satisfy vs in any thing we demand of them, by words or signes for their vnderstanding: neither haue they at any time beene at the least discord amongst themselues; insomuch as we haue not seen them angry, but merry; and so kinde, as if you giue any thing to one of them, he will distribute part of euery one of the rest.

[106] On the return trip they no doubt had fair winds directly astern and Gulf Stream currents to help them along. They averaged about 4.25 knots for the trip.

We haue brought them to vnderstand some English, and we vnderstand much of their language; so as we are able to aske them many things.[107] And this we haue observed, that if we shew them any thing, and ask them if they haue it in their countrey, they will tell you if they haue it, and the vse of it, the difference from ours in bignesse, colour, or forme: but if they haue it not, be it a thing neuer so precious, they will denie the knowledge of it.

They haue names for many starres, which they will show in the firmament.

They shew great reverence to their King, and are in great subiection to their Govenours: and they will shew a great respect to any we tell them are our Commanders.

---

[107] The reader should be careful not to take this to mean that there was actually an attempt on the part of Rosier to learn the language of his captives. It is obvious from remarks in several places in the narrative which indicate more a desire to get a description of their country and its bounty than understanding the people themselves.

It should also be remembered that knowledge of a list of vocabulary words does not constitute knowledge of a language. For instance, how does one understand the nature of such intangibles as spirits, events of the past, or seasons? The English interlocutors made such a hash of placenames that it has only been in recent years that linguists have been able to discover some of their errors, and the very document which probably came as a result of the questioning of these five Native Americans while in England (*Mawooshen*, Purchas, *Pilgrimes*, IV, 1625; XIX, XIX, p. 400), has yet to be successfully interpreted, even using present-day knowledge of Maine geography. Much of the confusion undoubtedly lies in the fact that even educated persons in England, at the time, spelled phonetically and often spelled the same word variably in the same sentence. With variations in English accent a word may have been pronounced entirely differently depending on how it was heard, or even which Indian said it. One notable example is Pemaquid which has appeared in various narratives of later voyages in various forms (Pemaquid, Pemaquyd, Bemoquid, Bemoquiducke, Pamma Quidda, Penaquida). Which incidentally, is the only attempt in Rosier's limited list at a geographical location and, as we know today, he misunderstood the Abenaki meaning, with the result that those who followed found Pemaquid in a completely different place.

They shew the maner how they make bread of their Indian wheat, and how they make butter and cheese of the milke they haue of the Rain-Deere and Fallo-Deere, which they haue tame as we haue Cowes.

They haue excellent colours. And hauing seen our Indico, they make shew of it, or of some other like thing which maketh as good blew.

One especiall thing is their maner of killing the Whale, which they call Powdawe; and will describe his forme; how he bloweth vp the water; and that he is 12 fathoms long; and that they go in company of their King with a multitude of their boats, and strike him with a bone made in fashion of a harping iron fastened to a rope, which they make great and strong of the barke of trees, which they veare out after him: then all their boats come about him, and as he riseth aboue water, with their arrowes they shoot him to death; when they haue killed him & dragged him to shore, they call all their chiefe lords together, & sing a song of ioy: and those chiefe lords, whom they call Sagamos, diuide the spoile, and giue to euery man a share, which pieces so distributed they hang vp about their houses for prouision; and when they boile them, they blow off the fat, and put to their peaze, maiz, and other pulse, which they eat.[108]

---

[108] There has been much controversy about the ability of the Native Americans to hunt and kill whales. To date, there has been no definitive evidence produced to resolve the issue. It must be said, however, that this description, unlike that of the deer which were milked like cows (!), contains a considerable amount of detail which, if not prompted or enhanced by the recorder, could easily be true. If any controversy exists as to whether a canoe is a suitable vehicle for whale hunting, it should be noted that many a whale boat was destroyed in the whale fishery, because of its large size, weight, and lack of maneuverability.

A briefe note of what profits we saw the Countrey yeeld in the small time of our stay there

TREES.
Oke of an excellent graine, strait, and great timber.
Elme.
Hazell.
Alder.
Cherry-tree.
Ash.
Maple.
Yew.
Spruce.
Aspe.
Firre.

Beech.
Birch, very tall and great; of whose barke they make their Canoas.
Wich-Hazell.
Many fruit trees, which we knew not.

FOWLES.
Penguins.
Crowes.
Sharks.
Rauens.
Mewes.
Turtle-Doues.
Many birds of sundrie
Many other fowls in flocks, vnknowen.

Eagles.
Hernshawes.
Cranes.
Ducks, great.
Geese.
Swannes.

BEASTS.
Raine-Deere.
Stagges.
Fallo-Deere.

Beares.
Wolues.
Beauer.
Otter.
Cony.
Hedge-Hoggs.
Polcats.
Wilde great Cats
Dogges: some like Wolues,
some like Spaniels.

FISHES.
Seales.
Cod very great.
Haddocke great.
Herring great.
Plaise.
Thornebacke.
Rockefish.
Soales.
Tortoises.
Oisters.

Lobster great.
Muscels great, with pearles
in them.
Cockles.
Wilks.
Cunner fish.
Lumps.
Whiting.

FRUITS, PLANTS and HERBS.
Wild-Vines.
Raspberries.
Tabacco, excellent sweet
and strong
Angelica, a most soueraigne
herbe.
An hearbe that spreadeth
the ground, & smelleth
like Sweet Marioram,
great plenty.

Strawberries.
Gooseberries.
Hurtleberries.
Currant trees.
Rose-bushes.
Peaze.
Ground-nuts.
Very good Dies, which
appeare by their
painting; which they
carrie with them in
bladders.

The names of the fiue Saluages which we brought home into England, which are all yet aliue, are these.

1. Tehanedo, a Sagamo or Commander.
2. Amoret
3. Skicowaros   Gentlemen.
4. Maneddo
5. Sassacomoit, a servant.

THREE

The Five Mawooshen Captives

T HE UNFORTUNATE FIVE — *Tehanedo, Amoret, Skicowaros, Maneddo,* and *Sassacomoit*—were taken to England on the return voyage. That first treacherous act, though not immediately revenged, forbode the constant mistrust that would plague English–Native relations for another century and a half.

Three of the five Indian captives, upon their arrival in England, were housed at the fort on Plymouth Hoe, then under the command of Sir Ferdinando Gorges. These, according to Gorges in his memoirs written many years later, were "Assacumet, Sketwarroes, and Manedy" (Gorges, 1658). Tehanedo, then being perceived as a sagamore, and perhaps more worthy in the eyes of a class-conscious English captor, was placed in the household of Sir John Popham, Lord Chief Justice of England. Of Amoret there is no further mention, although circumstances indicate his continued proximity to his brother, Tehanedo, probably also in the household of Popham.

In the spring of 1606, a follow-up voyage was planned in which two vessels would depart England for America and the place of Waymouth's discovery. The first of these, under the command of Captain Henry Challons, would be sponsored by Sir Ferdinando Gorges, and would leave in August. Two of Gorges's three captive Indians, Sassacomoit and Maneddo, along with John Stoneman, were aboard as guides. The second vessel, under the command of Captain Thomas Hanham, sponsored by Sir

John Popham, was to leave a short time later with Popham's two captive Indians, Tehanedo and Amoret. This vessel was to meet with Challons on the Maine Coast. The departure of these four captives for their homeland would leave only Skicowaros still in England in Gorges's household.

The *Richard*, Captain Challons's ship, never reached America. Captain Hanham did arrive on the Maine Coast and, failing to find the *Richard*, left Tehanedo and his brother Amoret in their village at what Hanham believed to be Pemaquid, and returned to England.

In 1607 another voyage was fitted out under the auspices of Sir Ferdinando Gorges and Sir John Popham, once again bound for the area explored by Waymouth in 1605, and presumably by Captain Hanham the year previous. This voyage, the now famous Popham Colony, carried Skicowaros, the last of the Waymouth captives. Almost immediately upon arriving on the Maine Coast he returned to his village, as had Tehanedo and Amoret. Based on events in later years it appears that at least two of these three lived long and eventful lives. Of the other two we know that in 1614 Sassacomoit was returned to his homeland by Captain Nicholas Hobson and not heard from again. Maneddo was only heard from with regard to the saga of the *Richard*, and it is likely that he died in Spain or England.

Tehanedo

While establishing their fort at Sagadahoc, George Popham and Raleigh Gilbert received several visits from Tehanedo and Skicowaros. On one such occasion, on September 8, 1607, "Captain Gilbert, with 22 others departed in the shallop for the River of Penobscot taking with him divers sortes of marchandizes to trade with the Bashaba...." Because of foul weather on that trip, Gilbert only made it as far east as their village, where he found no people at all. Here we have a good indication that the village Gilbert called Pemaquid had been, at least temporarily, perhaps seasonally, abandoned.

In the intervening years, between the events of 1607–08 and the explorations of Captain John Smith, in 1614, there is no record of what transpired on the coast. We get the sense, though, from customs records in England that fishing vessels coming and going at Pemaquid Harbor, Monhegan, and Damariscove Island must have been almost constant, and that much of the attitude held by both Mawooshen and English toward each other were formed by contact in those formative years. We do know that Francis Popham, the son of Sir John Popham, inherited from his father what remained of the Popham Colony at its breakup, and according to Captain John Smith and Sir Ferdinando Gorges, continued to send his ships to trade at Pemaquid (Smith, 1616).

On the last day of April 1614, Captain John Smith arrived on the coast with two vessels, the other captained by Thomas Hunt, and established Monhegan as his base of operation. There he briefly tried whaling, without success, and eventually set out with a crew of eight in a small boat, leaving Hunt and the rest to continue fishing. According to his own testimony, he was to have stayed in the country with sixteen others through the winter of 1614–15 to make a trial settlement. He apparently ranged the entire New England Coast from Penobscot Bay to Martha's Vineyard, mapping it as he proceeded, and traded with the Natives when he could. Although his narrative and map might cause one to presume that this was all done in great detail, he could not have stopped long at any one spot, for he had returned to Monhegan and set sail for England by 18 July—a stay of only two and one-half months all together. His stay had been cut short by the treachery of Hunt, who had taken anything of value from Smith's vessel and left before Smith's return to Monhegan. In his narrative we have another glimpse of the now famous Tehanedo and oblique mention of explosive conditions on the coast:

The maine assistance next God, I had to this small number [those seventeen men who, along with Smith, would have stayed through the winter], was my acquaintance among the salvages; especially with dohannida, one of their greatest lords; who had lived long in England. By the means of this proud salvage, I did not doubt but quickly to have gotte that credit with the rest of his friends, and alliants, to have had as many of them, as I desired in any design I intended, and that trade also they had, by such a kind of exchange of their countrie commodities; which both with ease and security in their seasons may be used. With him and diverse others, I had concluded to inhabit, and defend them against the Terentynes; with a better power than the French did them; whose tyranny did inforce them to imbrace my offer, with no small devotion.

Obviously Smith did not stay on the coast long enough to make good on his promise. If he had, and had lived to write the narrative we might now know the nature and result of the war that erupted the following year between the Mawooshen and the Terentynes (Indians of what is now New Brunswick).

Alas, we hear no more of Pemaquid for another ten years, long after the war had ended and most, if not all, of the Natives of the coast between the Penobscot and the Sagadahoc had been decimated or displaced to safer locations farther up the Kennebec. Indeed, those few years after Smith's visit were, based on what little has come down to us, tumultuous ones for the coastal Natives. Sir Ferdinando Gorges, in his *brief narration*, told of the exploratory voyage of Sir Richard Hawkins to the coast in October of 1615. In regard to the turmoil, he had this to say: "But the war was at the height, and the principle natives almost destroyed; so that his [Hawkins's] observation could not be such as could give account of any new matter, more than had been formerly received" (Gorges, 1658). We also know that the entire coast of New England was visited with a pandemic which decimated what population of the coast remained at the conclusion of the war. The nature of the disease and its origin are not known, but it has been speculated that it may have been transmitted from Europeans to the Native population.

The last glimpse we have of Tehanedo is on August 8, 1648. It is in the form of a deed from Monquin, alias Natahanada, to William Bradford of the Plymouth Colony for both sides of the Kennebec from Cushnoc (Augusta) to Wesserunskek (Skowhegan). In that deed he styled himself the son of "old Natowormet, Sachem of Kennebec river" (Statement of Kennebec Claims, Boston, 1786, 4-6). This is logical since *Mentaurmet* is described in the *Mawooshen* document of 1605 as the sagamore of *Nebamocago* (Indiantown Island, Boothbay). He is also given as *Manthoumermer* by Champlain on his 1605 excursion on the Sasanoa and Sheepscot Rivers, coincidentally at the same time which he was informed of an English ship's capture of five Indians. He was mentioned as *Menawormet* by Christopher Levett in 1623 at Capemanwagon. The indications in these sources are that Mentaurmet was an influential sagamore in the area from the Sagadahoc to Penobscot Bay with strong ties on the Kennebec. In 1623 Mentaurmet was at Indiantown Island and his sons Tehanedo and Amoret were still in the Pemaquid area. Certainly by 1648 "old Natowormet" was deceased, and all of the villages on the coast no longer existed, their populations having moved up the Kennebec. Tehanedo, along in years himself, was ceding territory on behalf of the remains of his people to the Plymouth Company, represented by William Bradford.

Amoret

That Amoret (styled by Purchas as "Bdahanedo's brother") was returned to America with Tehanedo is speculative, but probable, based on the pattern formed by Gorges and Popham. In fact, in this regard, it is too tempting not to mention the probability that he was *Samoset*. It was not unusual for printers to omit the initial or terminal letter of a word, apparently when none were left in the tray. In this case the letter would have been the initial *S*. Also, with the transposition of a lowercase *r* for an *s* while editing Rosier's manuscript, the name in Rosier's *Relation* would have been *Samoset*. This, of course, would have made Samoset Tehanado's brother, as well as "old Natowormet's son," something that would certainly explain Samoset's sagamore status and his ability to interact adroitly with Englishmen.

Samoset, of course, was one of New England's great heroic Indian characters. Several events in relation to his activities lead us to the conclusion that he resided at Muscongus, as had all of the Waymouth captives, increasing the likelihood that he was Rosier's Amoret. He first appears to us in the record of the Plymouth Colony, in its earliest months, and Governor Bradford's comment seems worth quoting:

> But about 16. of March a certaine Indian came bouldly amongst them, and spoke to them in broken English, which they could well understand, but marvelled at it. At length they understood by discourse with him, that he was not of these parts, but belonged to ye eastrene parts, wher some English-ships came to fhish, with whom he was aquainted, and could name sundrie of them by their names, amongst whom he had gott his language. He became profitable to them in aquainting them with many things concerning ye state of ye cuntry in ye east-parts wher he lived, which was afterwards profitable unto them; as also of ye people hear, of their names, number, strength; of their situation and distance from this place, and who was chief amongst them. His name was Samaset (Bradford, 1647).

Governor Bradford's statement that Samoset had learned English from the fishermen at the "eastrene parts" indicates that he had not been told of a visit to England. The "eastrene parts" can be nowhere but Monhegan and Pemaquid. Bradford's view notwithstanding, apparently by 1620 Samoset's English was excellent, having had a strong beginning with Rosier, and developing further in Sir John Popham's household in England.

Samoset next showed up in the Damariscotta River area in the late fall of 1623, where he and several others greeted Captain Christopher Levett, whose account concerning the Pemaquid area follows:

The next place I came to was Capemanwagan, a place where nine ships fished this yeare. But I like it not for a plantation, for I could see little good timber & lesse good ground, there I staid foure nights, in which time, there came many Savages with their wives and children, and some of good accompt amongst them, as Menawormet a Sagamore, Cogawesco the Sagamore of Casco and Quack, now called Yorke, Somerset, a Sagamore, one that hath ben found very faithful to the English, and hath saved the lives of many of our nation, some from starving, others from killing.

They intended to have been gone presently, but hearing of my being there, they desired to see me which I understood by one of the Masters of the ships, who likewise told me that they had some store of Beaver coats and skinnes, and was going to Pemaquid to truck with one Mr. Witheridge, a Master of a ship of Bastable, and desired me to use meanes that they should not carry them out of the harbour, I wisht them to bring all their truck to one Mr. Cokes stage, & I would do the best I could to put it away: some of them did accordingly, and I then sent for the Sagamores, who came, and after some compliments they told me I must be their cozen, and that Captain Gorges was so, (which you can imagine I was a little proud of, to be adopted cozen to so many great Kings at one instant, but did willingly accept of it) and so passing away a little time very pleasantly, they desired to be gone, whereupon I told them that I ynderstood they had some coates and Beavers skins which I desired to truck for but they were unwilling, and I seemed carelesse of it (as men must do if they desire any thing of them). But at last Somerset swore that there should be none carryed out of the harbour, but his cozen Levett should have all, and then they began to offer me some by way of gift, but I would take none but one pair of sleeves from Cogawesco, but told them it was not the fashion of English Captaines alwaies to be taking, but sometimes to take and give, and continually truck was very good. But in fine, we had all except one coate and two skinnes, which they reserved to pay an old debt with, but they staying all that night, had them stole from them.

As Capemanwagon was a name used for Southport Island, it seems likely that this encounter took place in the vicinity of Damariscove and Fisherman Islands where staging areas had, for many years, been set up on the open ledges by certain proprietors for the purpose of air drying salted fish before transporting to Europe and England. The vain and naive Captain Levett, through his audacious, but attentive, manner managed to win over the savvy, and no doubt cynical, Native sagamores, and to succeed at trade. He apparently didn't make it as far east as Pemaquid, the next peninsula, but instead returned to House Island in Portland Harbor, where he set up residence.

Little more is known of Samoset (or Amoret) except where his name and mark appear in the sale of lands in the vicinity of the Pemaquid Peninsula, Bremen, and Waldoboro. A famous deed of land to John Brown of New Harbor dated 15 July 1625 was one such instrument. Another was a deed of land (a part of which had already been contained in John Brown's deed) in the vicinity of Round Pond and New Harbor to Richard Pearce, John Brown's son-in-law, dated 9 January 1641. The first of these was controversial from 1734 until recently, when it has been declared an eighteenth-century forgery (Edwin A. Churchill, *Introduction to Archeological Excavations at Pemaquid, Maine*, Helen B. Camp, 1974, p. ix). Sometime in the mid-nineteenth century Mr. J. Wingate Thornton discovered a manuscript deed of land transferred by "Captaine Sommarset" to a William Parnall, Thomas Way, and William England, written in July 1653 (Maine Historical Society *Collections*, Second Series, V, p. 188). At that time Samoset would have been well along in years and his ultimate fate is lost to history.

Skicowaros

The last of the five Waymouth captives to be sent from England was Skicowaros. He was put aboard Raleigh Gilbert's ship, *Gift of God*, and made part of the so-called Popham and Gilbert voyage which started the ill-fated Popham Colony in 1607. He had been housed at Plymouth Fort with Sir Ferdinando Gorges from August 1605 to the departure of the Popham Colony in the fall of 1607. After arriving on the Maine Coast he returned to his village. He is mentioned several times in the accounts of the colony, along with Tehanedo, but so far as is known, from 1607 onward he is not mentioned again.

Sassacomoit

The story of Sassacomoit, if we knew it all, would surely make as fascinating reading as Samoset's, but because of the lack of available detail, we must be content with an abreviated version here. His story began with his capture by Waymouth in 1605. Within a year of Waymouth's return to England, Henry Challons was dispatched to North Virginia with Maneddo and Assacomoit aboard as Native guides. The voyage went awry when Challons ventured south into the West Indies and was captured by a Spanish squadron. In the scuffle Sassacomoit was badly injured, but survived. The entire company was taken to Seville where Challons and most of his company, including Maneddo and Sassacomoit, were imprisoned. Through much diplomatic finagling most were eventually returned to England where Sassacomoit was received back into Sir Ferdinando Gorges's household for the second time.

Upon his return from Spain to England sometime in 1608, Sassacomoit apparently resided as a servant in the household of Sir Ferdinando Gorges, where he, no doubt, learned to speak very good English. He also, no doubt, imparted much information about his native country of the *Mawooshen*, thereby keeping Sir Ferdinando Gorges's interest in the New World piqued. In 1614 Gorges sent Captain Nicholas Hobson to explore the coast of New England yet again. After nine years of captivity, Sassacomoit was included on that voyage. Gorges's brief account of the voyage fails to note whether Sassacomoit was returned to his native village or not, and his name is then lost to us.

Maneddo

Maneddo stayed in England from Waymouth's return in August 1605 until August 1606. He then was sent along on Captain Challons's misadventure. Although the ship and most of its crew were repatriated to England in 1608 after much adventure in Spain, Maneddo was not mentioned in that, or any other context, again. It is presumed that he died in Spain or in England.

FOUR

The Continuing Controversy

C APTAIN GEORGE WAYMOUTH and James Rosier, at the end of their discovery, quickly left the scene. In fact, all of the participants in the enterprise, with the exception of one, were displaced by a new cast of characters. The only member of the Waymouth discovery crew to remain employed by the new promoters and backers was John Stoneman (probably a master's mate and assistant to Thomas Cam aboard *Archangell*), retained to be the pilot in the first ensuing voyage to the location of Waymouth's discovery. We now know that, by a later accident of fate, John Stoneman, too was displaced, leaving the exact location of Waymouth's discovery in question.

Statements made in early seventeenth-century sources subsequent to the Waymouth voyage do not indicate any recognition of Waymouth's discovery of the Penobscot River. In fact, the evidence of subsequent settlement activity to the westward, despite a clear and unambiguous narrative, seems to fly in the face of any claim for that discovery, and has led to much speculation and controversy since. This discrepancy cannot be resolved by any of the later narratives, which have either been destroyed or are silent on the matter. This we believe to be the "elephant in the parlor" which historians have been attempting to explain since the sevententh century.

The controversy continued into the nineteenth century. The issues were not adequately resolved by historians, and could not be, without partisan influence on the result. The voyage, and its effect on American settlement, therefore, could not be defined and described with any certainty. As a result Waymouth, Rosier, and their legacy were relegated to the record as a minor footnote in the history of New England.

Four hundred years have passed and the political and religious issues of the time have faded, along with the Native population displaced by their effects. We are left today with only the seemingly petty controversy about which river James Rosier described. Some have argued that this issue was truly only a footnote in the early seventeenth century, and is, therefore, even less relevant today. Nothing could be further from the truth. In the summers of 1604 and 1605 two explorers entered a great river on the Maine Coast, described by both in narratives which still exist. One was English and one was French. One was George Waymouth and the other was Samuel de Champlain. Although he apparently made no claim to it, Champlain's river is unarguably the Penobscot. Waymouth's river, on which he made a claim for England, has been in question for four hundred years. Based wholly on information from the exploration of George Waymouth, at least three English voyages were immediately sent to the Maine Coast in 1606 and 1607, all having colonists aboard, bound for the location of Waymouth's discovery.

Today, the questions we ask are these: Were both of those discoveries on the Penobscot River? If so, how much effect did the unknowing abandonment of that claim by the English settling on the Sagadahoc River in 1607, rather than the Penobscot, have on French claims, claims which resulted in turmoil and upheaval experienced by the Natives, the English, and the French in America throughout the seventeenth and eighteenth centuries? How much different would our subsequent history be if the Virginia Company's follow-up voyages had settled on the Penobscot?

Having answers to those questions now will certainly not change events of the past four hundred years. It is our obligation, nevertheless, to examine the premise with new evidence, as well as to reassess the old, in order to update the record.

The Ironies

Because of its importance to Maine's, and New England's, earliest history, it is truly unfortunate that the Waymouth voyage brought with it so many ironies, and that those ironies began to be in play at the conception of the voyage. The first, perhaps, is that although the purpose of the voyage was approved by England's King James I, there was a subsequent conflict, removing its original promoter from the process before the return of the voyage. The second is that Waymouth discovered a place to which he originally was not bound, and for all practical purposes was unknown by the English. The third is that Waymouth and Rosier were displaced as soon as the voyage was ended. The fourth is the loss of the Challons voyage as a follow-up to Waymouth's, where John Stoneman, who had been with Waymouth, would have provided the knowledge of exactly where Waymouth had been. The fifth is the probable discarding of the manuscript records of the Hanham voyage by Samuel Purchas. The sixth is the fact that Waymouth's positively identifiable Pentecost Harbor is located six miles from the mainland where few historians involved in the controversy would be able to see Waymouth's geographic viewpoint. The seventh is the phonetic similarity of the Abenaki compound words, *Pem-akwek* and *Pemi-keag*.

Bemoquiducke and Pemaquid

The last of these ironies involves the English evolution of an unwritten Mawooshen compound word heard by Rosier as *Bemoquiducke*. This term evolved into *Pamma Quidda*, and eventually to *Pemaquid*, as heard and recorded by other Englishmen. It seems that its English misunderstanding occurred between 1605 and 1606. That misunderstanding forms the basis on which we contend the Penobscot River was unknowingly abandoned by the Virginia Company in 1607, with far-reaching effects on English colonial settlement in America.

James Rosier, at the end of his *Relation* recording Waymouth's voyage, said that he had gathered a list of terms which he acquired from some of the Natives who visited *Archangell* at Pentecost Harbor, numbering some four or five hundred words. Although he didn't include them, Samuel Purchas published a handful in 1625 from the Rosier manuscripts he inherited from Richard Hakluyt. One of the listed terms and its translation is, "The maine Land, *Bemoquiducke*."

To see how Rosier arrived at his translation we must take into consideration that he had no understanding of the dialect he was hearing, and that he certainly had to get these terms by pointing to the object, or in the direction of the place being considered. If, aboard *Archangell* at Burnt Island, he pointed to the mainland to the northeast, within his view, and the Native to whom he queried thought that he was asking for the name of the Camden Hills in that same direction, he would have received the word *Pemakwek*, with the locative ending *-uk*. With some phonetic confusion Rosier's understanding of the term *Pem-akwek-uk* was that it meant area of "the maine Land" in a northeasterly direction from the anchorage at Burnt Island, which he, no doubt, wrote into his notes.

During the interrogation of the captives in England, at least one of those Natives related much of the information given in a remarkable document titled *The Description of the Countrey of Mawooshen*. This description, perhaps part of a much larger version compiled by Sir Ferdinando Gorges or Richard Hakluyt, was first printed by Samuel Purchas in *Purchas His Pilgrimes* (Purchas, 1625). The subchapter head was this: *The description of the Countrey of Mawooshen, discouered by the English, in the yeere 1602. 3. 5. 6. 7. 8. and 9.* A sidebar at the first paragraph states, "This description of Mawooshen I had amongst M[aster]. Hakluyts papers." Although the information was probably compiled as early as the fall of 1605, Purchas's edited version was not printed until 1625. His references to the English discoveries were:

1602...Voyage of Bartholomew Gosnold to Cape Cod
1603...Voyage of Martin Pring to Cape Ann and Cape Cod

1605...Voyage of George Waymouth to the Maine Coast
1606...Aborted voyage of Challons, Hind, and Stoneman bound for *Pamma-quidda* in *Mayaushon*
1606...Voyage of Thomas Hanham & Martin Pring to the Maine Coast
1607...Voyage of Popham & Gilbert to Sagadahoc (Popham Colony)
1608...Voyage for the return of the survivors of the Popham Colony
1609...not recorded

The *Description of the Countrey of Mawooshen*, at the time of its compilation shortly after Waymouth's voyage, was an Englishman's attempt to put in writing the names of all the known rivers that could be encountered on the coast along with the names of the Native villages on them, their sagamores, and their population. In the document there are eleven rivers, twenty-one villages, and twenty-four sagamores named—the entire Mawooshen homeland comprising most of the state of Maine as we know it today. These watersheds are described in a sequence beginning with the Union River on the east and ending with the Saco River on the west.

It is obvious, once again, based on the translation of the term, that the compiler, having no knowledge of the dialect he was hearing, misunderstood *Mawooshen*, a term of ethnicity which described a cultural group of Native people as "hunters." He thought Mawooshen to be a place, or country. However confused the interrogator may have been about the true meaning of the terms he was soliciting, we now know that the understanding by the young Native about what was being asked caused him to be accurate and consistent in his responses.

Because these aboriginal people used no proper nouns, they simply named a prominent feature of the place they were describing. In each case when they were asked to name a river, it would have been impossible to sum up all the features of a watershed with one word. In this case the Native narrator, who understood the question perfectly, chose to give the name of a uniquely prominent feature of that particular river, as it could be seen and understood from the vantage point of an Englishman aboard his vessel. The Native who gave us *The Description of the Countrey of Mawooshen* used a compound word, in his language, to describe the entrance to what we now call the Penobscot River.

The word, heard as *Bemoquiducke* by Rosier, and interpreted as "the maine Land" was also heard as *Pemaquid* by the English editor of the *Mawooshen* document, and interpreted as the proper name of a river, specifically the one we now call the Penobscot. Both are incorrect, and give us some indication of the misunderstanding, which in 1605, was looming. The compound word which they both certainly heard was *Pem-akwek-uk* and *Pem-akwek*, which are both the same, one with the locative *-uk*. The compound word is derived from two roots, *Pem-* or *Pemi-*, roughly meaning "extended, continuous (on and on), or lengthened," and *-akwek*, sometimes *akwek-uk*, meaning "height, steep place, or hill" (Laurent, 1995, pp. 138, 293; also Eckstorm, 1941, pp. 3, 22). The full word, therefore, translates to "extended steep hill." The only place of an extended steep hill is the Camden Hills, which are prominently visible as an extended series of hills from every vantage point when sailing by or entering Penobscot Bay. Here we can see the same word used by two Native people to describe the same place, the Camden Hills, but misunderstood by two English recorders.

Stoneman's Voyage to Pamma Quidda in Mayushon

As a result of Waymouth's voyage and the information received from his Indian captives, plans for establishing a colony on the coast generated much enthusiasm, and preparations for another voyage were set in motion (Gorges, 1659). The plan called for two ships to sail separately from England, to the place of Waymouth's discoveries. Captain Henry Challons was to command the *Richard*, with Nicholas Hind as master, and John Stoneman along as pilot. Two of Waymouth's captured Natives, Sassacomoit and Maneddo, would go along as interpreters and guides to help Stoneman. A group of merchants and colonists were present to be the beginning of a new colony. Starting later, Thomas Hanham was to command the second vessel (the ship's name is now lost), with Martin Pring as master. Another of Waymouth's captives, Tehanedo, and probably his brother Amoret, were included in Hanham's complement, along with more prospective colonists.

According to a later deposition given by Nicholas Hind, the sailing master of Captain Challons's vessel, the destination of these voyages was "Pamma Quidda in Mayushon" (P.R.O., HCA 14/38). This is a reference to the English interest in returning to the place where Rosier recorded Waymouth's discoveries, and to form an English settlement there (Gorges, 1659). The *Richard* was to go ahead to establish the *Pem-akwek-uk* location, using the knowledge of Stoneman, with Sassacomoit and Maneddo to help guide and interpret. Hanham's vessel was to follow in a matter of days. The plan was put into motion and the *Richard* sailed for America. From that point, however, much of the evidence has been lost and what remains is very subtle. The *Richard*, with her commander (Challons), sailing master (Hind), pilot (Stoneman), and crew was captured by a Spanish squadron and taken to Spain, never to arrive in America. The aborted voyage is well documented in records of the legal maneuverings between England and Spain, concerning repatriation of the ship and its crew.

The failure of the *Richard*, and especially Stoneman, to reach America effectively eliminated anyone with firsthand knowledge of the specific location of Waymouth's discovery, and left the voyage of Hanham and Pring to the guidance of Tehanedo for information about their ultimate destination. We know that a record of the voyage made by Hanham existed, but was destroyed (Purchas, 1625). We also know, by statements of Ferdinando Gorges, their backer, that they arrived on the coast, and failing to meet with the Challons group, made some explorations, left Tehanedo in his homeland, and returned to England (Gorges, 1659). We can only suppose that Tehanedo, in Stoneman's absence, was easily able to convince Hanham that *Pem-akwek-uk* (Bemoquiducke, Pamma Quidda, Pemaquid) was the mainland nearest his village on the present-day Pemaquid Peninsula. His interest was in getting home, and if that meant letting the Englishmen understand it as Pemaquid, can we blame him? He certainly would have had no interest in the promotion of Waymouth's discovery. This very subtle misunderstanding then became accepted by all who ever returned to that coastal vicinity.

By 1616, when Captain John Smith wrote his *History of New England*, he mentioned Pemaquid twice in connection with its present-day location and renamed it St. Johns Towne. Because the fishing vessels of Sir Ferdinando Gorges, Sir Francis Popham, and others, returned to Monhegan and Damariscove where they dried their catches year after year from 1610 onward, the misnomer became thoroughly embedded in English colonial geography and terminology.

Pemi-keag

Ironically, there is another Abenaki compound term that, heard by a different ear, could be mistaken for *Pem-akwek*. Fannie Hardy Eckstorm, following other scholars, interpreted Pemaquid as meaning "long point" or "a point of land running into the sea" (Eckstorm, 1941, p. 102). Mrs. Eckstorm, and those she quoted, based their interpretation on two roots, the first of which is *Pem* or *Pemi-*, as explained above. The second, however, is *-keag*, which is the noun "point," being a point of land extending into a river or the ocean. It is understandable, and logical, that these scholars would interpret the word that sounds like "Pemaquid" as "long point," especially if they already knew that Pemaquid had been the English proper name of a peninsula below Damariscotta since 1606. The arguments opposing this *Pemi-keag* interpretation for the place of Waymouth's discovery are threefold: First, "long point" is ubiquitous on the Maine Coast; second, the *Description of the Countrey of Mawooshen*, a remarkably consistent document, logically gives the geographic location, *Pemaquid*, to describe a

[114]

feature of the Penobscot River, not a point such as the Pemaquid Peninsula; and third, the Penobscot River is the only river on the Maine Coast that can even vaguely match the geographic descriptions in Rosier's narrative.

We also believe that these very similar phonemes, *Pem-akwek* and *Pemi-keag* can explain why Natives Tehanedo and others, did not correct the Englishmen who, mistakenly, sought *Pamma-Quidda* at the present day Pemaquid peninsula. If Stoneman had been present, phonetic similarities would have been moot, since his knowledge of Waymouth's discovery would have prevailed, in any case.

The Simancus Map

At this point in the controversy it seems necessary to revisit and, hopefully, put to rest some of the arguments raised in favor of the St. George River as Waymouth's discovery. Some of these issues were proffered more than one hundred years ago, and to many are still relevant.

The Simancus Map is a remarkably detailed representation of the East Coast of North America from Chesapeake Bay to the northern tip of Newfoundland, with features from English, Dutch, and French sources. In 1610 it contained most of the existing geographical knowledge of the area covered and is, today, a valuable historic document. It contains absolutely nothing, however, that can be definitively attributed to George Waymouth. The river labeled Tahanock could as easily be the Damariscotta River as the St. George River, and the word *Tahanock*, presumably Native although no other use of the term has been found anywhere else, gives us no clue whatever. The presence of the river and cross on a map of 1610 only indicates discovery of the river prior to 1610.

Several explorations could have provided this information. Hanham and Pring explored the coast in 1606 and Hanham's journal from that voyage is known to have existed in England but was destroyed, unpublished, by Samuel Purchas. Purchas did, however, publish a brief synopsis of a few of the voyages to New England from 1607 to 1622, as recorded by a member of the

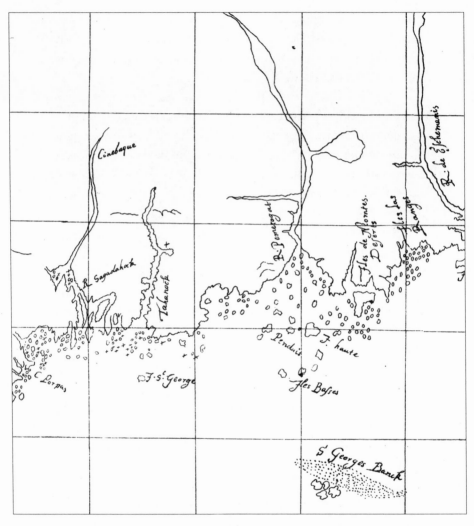

The Simancus Map

Council for New England, perhaps Sir Ferdinando Gorges (Purchas, 1625). The statements concerning the Hanham voyage are worth noting:

> This losse [the Challons voyage], and unfortunate beginning, did much abate the rising courage of the first adventurers; but immediately upon his [Challons's] departure, it pleased the noble Lord Chief Justice, Sir John Popham Knight, to send out another shippe, wherein Captayne Thomas Hanam went commander, and Martine Prinne of Bristow Master, with all necessary supplyes, for the seconding of Captayne Challons and his people; who arriving at the place appointed, and not finding that Captayne there, after they had made some Discoverie, and found the Coasts, Havens, and Harbours answerable to our desires, they returned. Upon whose Relation the Lord Chief Justice, and we all waxed so confident of the businesse, that the yeere following every man of any worth [financial], formerly interested in it, was willing to join in the charge [cost] for sending over a competent number of people to lay the ground of a hopeful Plantation.

As we have said, these two voyages were intended to be a follow-up to the voyage of Waymouth and the statement "made some Discoverie, and found the Coasts, Havens, and Harbours answerable to our desires" seems to indicate that goal, as well as new explorations in the area, as well. The Popham Colony was, as we know, the "hopeful Plantation."

Certainly Raleigh Gilbert had many opportunities to explore the area during the stay of the Popham Colony in 1607–08, as well. Purchas, in his *Mawooshen* document, also listed a 1609 voyage, of which, due to his admitted carelessness, we have no record.

Finally, with regard to the Simancus Map, the cross, interestingly the only one on the map, if contemporary could as easily have been an x, intended by Hanham to be put under discussion upon his return as a possible site for the Popham Colony. This, of course, is pure supposition, but it should be sufficient to illustrate the point that the Simancas Map is not conclusive evidence of anything in the case of Captain George Waymouth's voyage.

The Magnitude of the River

The St. George River, however proximate to Waymouth's activities, cannot begin to match Rosier's description, either in regard to times and distances traveled or the magnitude of its resources. To view the Penobscot River from the same vantage point, at the same time of year, even today, allows one to appreciate Rosier's enthusiasm. It is on this argument that the proponents of the Penobscot River have rested their case for many years.

Rosier's narrative gives quite clearly the distances traveled and comments on soundings on both of Waymouth's expeditions up the river. These distances are far in excess of any possible travel on the St. George, and require speculation beyond the ability of the narrative to support it. It must be said that Rosier, if taken at his word, is precise about what he has omitted: "And this is the cause that I have neither written of the latitude or variation most exactly observed by our Captaine...." As stated, he has clearly omitted precise navigational entries, such as latitudes, in order to avoid divulging the exact location of the discovery. He refers to omissions, not misstatements. It is easy to dismiss specific statements in the narrative as politically motivated, deliberate misrepresentations. The difficulty with that argument is this: if Rosier cannot be taken at his word at any one point in the narrative, we invite the rejection of his entire account.

Conclusion

The principal inheritors of the Waymouth enterprise from Arundel were Sir Ferdinando Gorges, Sir John Popham, and their associates whose primary interest was to continue the original goal of transporting a colony of English citizens to America. To accomplish this, the following year, 1606, they each undertook, at their own expense, to send a vessel to the specific location of Waymouth's discovery. As we now know, the first of those ships never arrived, and, although the second did, its activities and the locations of those activities are unknown to us. Because it returned to England without leaving the complement of colonists it carried, this voyage, too, failed in its larger mission.

Undeterred by the complete loss of one ship, but perhaps encouraged by information (or, as we suggest, misinformation) supplied by the other, Gorges and Popham undertook an even more ambitious voyage. Under the command of Captains George Popham and Raleigh Gilbert, the goal again was to arrive at what all believed was Waymouth's Bemoquiducke (Pamma Quidda), and from there proceed to a suitable location for the building of a fortified community. They found Pemaquid to be four leagues to the west of Waymouth's Pentecost Harbor, which they had identified by Waymouth's cross. Misinformation, conveyed by some means, in 1606 had placed Waymouth's Bemoquiducke twelve miles west of Pentecost Harbor when, based on evidence in Rosier's account, it was, in fact, twenty-six miles to the northeast. The colony we now know as the Popham Colony was established on a cold, barren, granite outcrop at the mouth of the Kennebec River (perhaps under the assumption, even then, that the Sagadahoc was the great river of Rosier's description) and Waymouth's Penobscot River was abandoned by the English.

The period following Waymouth's voyage, until 1620, saw the formative beginnings of the establishment of the English people on American soil. It was the legitimate opportunity, based on John Cabot's discovery of Newfoundland, in 1497, for Englishmen to secure for their nation and their religion a place in the New World, regardless of the claims of Spain, France, and the Roman Church. From the incorporation of the North and South Colonies of Virginia under that English claim onward, the organizers of the South Colony, through wealth and liberal influence in London, were able to vigorously proceed with their efforts to settle Jamestown. The North Colony, on the other hand, through the high-minded, aristocratic bungling of its founders and voyage captains, was only able to produce the abortive Popham Colony—we would argue, to use a variation on a recently popular phrase—by the wrong people, in the wrong place, at the wrong time.

It is difficult to argue that the mere absence of a 1607 English settlement at Camden, on Penobscot Bay, would have changed the dynamics of Native, English, and French relations for such a long time in America's formative period. It is a fact, nevertheless, that the ambivalence of the English Crown concerning the limits of its claims east of the Kennebec River allowed a very small number of French traders and Jesuits, using the Penobscot both as an outpost and a highway to Canada, to hold sway over the entire maritime peninsula for the next 158 years.

There were many factors, besides the absence of a well-fortified, viable English population, which allowed those conditions to exist. Others were: the English arrogance toward the Native population, as exemplified by Waymouth's behavior; French influence and control, through Jesuits, of the Native population; efforts in the English Parliament to undermine the claims of Gorges, Popham, and their partners favored by the Crown; and lack of interest in, and the periodic use of, the Penobscot River as a pawn in treaty negotiations with France until the Treaty of Paris in 1763. We would argue, however, that the first and greatest English misstep in the plan for the long-term, peaceful settlement of the Maine Coast was the failure of Henry Challons, Thomas Hanham, George Popham, and Raleigh Gilbert to accomplish the goals set out for them by Sir Ferdinando Gorges and Sir John Popham—to settle Waymouth's Penobscot River.

A Chronology

DAY	DATE	TIME	EVENT
Tuesday	5 March	10 A.M.	Set sail from Ratcliffe (in the Thames River)
Sunday	10 March	Night	Anchored in the Downes (mouth of the Thames)
Monday	11 March	3 P.M.	Set sail
Saturday	16 March	4 P.M.	Anchored at Dartmouth Haven
Sunday	31 March	5 P.M.	Weighed anchor and set sail from England
Monday	1 April	6 A.M.	Six leagues south of the Lizard (southernmost point of England)
Monday	1 April	2 P.M.	Sounded in 56½ fathoms
Sunday	14 April	9–10 A.M.	Sighted the Island of Corvo (Azores)
Monday	6 May	10 A.M.	Latitude 39½°N, Came to a rippling
Monday	13 May	11 A.M.	Sounded in 160 fathoms
Monday	13 May	4 P.M.	Sounded in 100 fathoms
Monday	13 May	10 P.M.	Took in all sails
Tuesday	14 May	3 A.M.	Set sails and sounded in 100 fathoms
Tuesday	14 May	8 A.M.	Sounded in 5 fathoms, sighted a white sandy cliff west-north-west, six leagues (18 miles) away

Tuesday	14 May	Night	Stood off and attempted to sail southward
Wednesday	15 May	Night	Failed to make headway southward, turned north
Thursday	16 May	Not stated	Stood in toward the land where he perceived it to be
Friday	17 May	6 P.M.	Sighted land to the north-north-east, stood off again
Saturday	18 May	2 A.M.	Stood in toward the land
Saturday	18 May	8 A.M.	Sighted land again, bearing northeast
Saturday	18 May	12 Noon	Anchored 1 league (3 miles) north of Monhegan
Saturday	18 May	2 P.M.	Went ashore, gathered wood, returned to the ship
Sunday	19 May	12 Noon	Weighed anchor and stood in to the Georges Islands
Sunday	19 May	4 P.M.	Anchored in Pentecost Harbor
Monday	20 May	Early A.M.	Put pieces of the pinnace ashore, began digging wells
Monday	20 May	Daytime	Fished about a mile from the ship
Monday	20 May	Evening	Cast a net for fish
Wednesday	22 May	All day	Cut wood, scoured wells, planted a garden with peas and barley
Friday	24 May	Daytime	Explored Allen and Benner Islands
Wednesday	29 May	Not stated	Finished the shallop, set up a cross on the shore
Thursday	30 May	10 A.M.	Captain Waymouth and 14 others left in shallop

Thursday	30 May	5 P.M.	Three canoes arrived (the first Natives seen)
Friday	31 May	Very early	Three Natives came aboard
Friday	31 May	10 A.M.	Captain Waymouth arrived from 40-mile exploration
Saturday	1 June	Forenoon	Rosier traded with Natives (28 altogether)
Saturday	1 June	Evening	Captain Waymouth fished with a seine net
Saturday	1 June	Night	Owen Griffin slept ashore with Indians
Sunday	2 June	Sunrise	5 or 6 canoes arrivef, Rosier sent them away
Sunday	2 June	5 P.M.	3 canoes arrived from the mainland
Monday	3 June	Early	Captain Waymouth with 15 others, including Rosier, followed two canoes in the Light Horseman to the mainland
Tuesday	4 June	8 A.M.	Captain Waymouth went ashore for wood and water, 2 canoes arrived with 6 Natives; Waymouth, Rosier, and crew captured five with canoes and all bows and arrows, one escaped into the woods
Wednesday	5 June	All day	Brought aboard firewood and filled their great water cask
Thursday	6 June	All day	Carefully stowed canoes and Natives below decks
Saturday	8 June	Very early	Captain Waymouth sounded about the islands adjoining, found a pond of fresh water hard by the shore

Saturday	8 June	1 P.M.	2 canoes arrived fron the east-ward, sent from the Bashebas, with invitation to bring the ship to his village upon the mainland towards the east
Tuesday	11 June	Not stated	Archangell sailed up into the river 26 miles
Wednesday	12 June	Not stated	Captain Waymouth with 17 men rowed up to the codde of the river, went ashore and marched over three hills in order to get to a mountain
Wednesday	12 June	Upon return	3 Natives in 1 canoe arrived at the ship at anchor
Wednesday	12 June	?	At this point there appears to be a journal entry missing as the vessel must have been moved upriver about 14 miles
Thursday	13 June	2 A.M.	Captain Waymouth and Light Horseman crew left ship at anchor, rowed to that part of the river that trended westward
Thursday	13 June	Before light	Arrived at the point mentioned above and left cross
Thursday	13 June	Before light	Started rowing up the river, rowed to Brewer, and back to *Archangell*
Friday	14 June	4 A.M.	*Archangell* was sailed and towed by the shallop and ship's boat down to the mouth of the river; afterward the captain explored the mouth of the river

Saturday	15 June	Not stated	Weighed anchor and sailed from the mouth of the river to Pentecost Harbor
Sunday	16 June	Not stated	Weighed anchor and sailed from Pentecost Harbor for England
Tuesday	18 June	After 4 P.M.	Sounded in 24 fathoms, took down sails and fished
Sunday	14 July	6 P.M.	Arrived in the English Channel
Tuesday	16 July	5 A.M.	Passed Scylly
Thursday	18 July	4 P.M.	Entered Dartmouth Haven

References

Andrews, Kenneth R. *English Privateering Voyages to the West Indies 1589–95*. Cambridge, 1959. Hakluyt Society, Second Series, III.
_____. *English Voyages to the Carribean, 1596 to 1604*. In *William and Mary Quarterly*, Third Series, vol. 31, no. 2, April 1974.

Archer, Gabriel. *The relation of Captaine Gosnols Voyage to the North part of Virginia, begunne the sixe and twentieth of March, Anno 42. Elizabethae Reginae 1602*. In Samuel Purchas, *Purchas his Pilgrimes*, IV (1625), 1647–51. Hakluyt Society, XVII (1906), 303–13.
_____. *The relation of Captain Gosnolds Voyage*. In H. S. Burrage, *Early English and French Voyages: Chiefly from Hakluyt, 1534–1608*, NY, Charles Scribner's Sons, 1906, 330–39.

Aubery, Father Joseph. *French Abenaki Dictionary*. From the manuscript of Father Joseph O'Brien which was hand copied from the original manuscript of Father Aubery (c. 1715). With English translation by Stephen Laurent, Maine Historical Society, Portland, 1995. Note: This is the only printed version of this important dictionary. This work was originally compiled by Father Aubery at St. Francis in 1715, making it the earliest dictionary of the Abenaki dialect recorded. Fannie Hardy Eckstorm said of Aubery that he "knew perfectly the Abnaki dialect" and characterized this work (only in manuscript form at the time) as "the most scholarly Jesuit compilation the present writer [Eckstorm] knows" (Eckstorm, 1941).

Baker, William A. *Colonial Vessels*. Barre, MA, 1962
_____. *Sloops and Shallops*. Barre, MA, Barre Publishing Co., 1966

Ballard, Edward, ed. *Popham Memorial Volume*. Portland, ME, Bailey & Noyes, 1860

Baxter, James Phinney, ed. *The life and letters of Sir Ferdinando Gorges*. 3 vols., Boston, 1890, Prince Society Publications, 18–20. Reprinted NY, 1967.

Beer, George Lewis. *The Origins of the British Colonial System 1578–1660*. NY, The Macmillan Company, 1922.

Belknap, Jeremy, D. D., ed.*Captain George Waymouth*. In *American Biography: or, an Historical Account of Those Persons Who Have Been Distinguished in America, as Adventurers, Statesmen, Philosophers, Divines, Warriors, Authors, and Other Remarkable Characters. Comprehending a Recital of the Events Connected With their Lives and Actions...*, Boston, Isaiah Thomas and Ebenezer T. Andrews, MDCCXCIV–VIII, 2 vols.

Biggar, Henry P., ed. *Samuel de Champlain, Works*. 6 vols. and portfolio, Toronto, 1922–36, Champlain Society Publications, New Series, 1–6, and portfolio; reprinted, Toronto, 1971, 7 vols.

Bourne, William. *A regiment of the sea*. Edited by Eva G. R. Taylor, Hakluyt Society, Second Series, No. 121, 1963.

Brereton, John. *A briefe and true relation of the Discoverie of the North part of Virginia*. Facsimile of the 1602 first edition, with notes by Luther S. Livingston, NY, 1903.
_____. *A briefe and true relation*. In H.S. Burrage, *English and French Voyages, 1534–1608*, NY, Charles Scribner's Sons, 1906, 325–40.
_____. *A Briefe and true relation.*, in D. B. Quinn, *New American World*, III, NY, Arno Press and Hector Bye, Inc., 1979; London, MacMillan, 1979, 347–52.

Burrage, Henry S., ed. *Rosier's Relation of Waymouth's Voyage to the Coast of Maine, 1605*. The Gorges Society, Portland, 1887.
_____ *Early English and French Voyages, 1534–1608*. NY, 1906; reprinted, 1969, Charles Scribner's Sons.
_____. *The beginnings of colonial Maine*. Portland, ME, 1914. Printed for the State of Maine.
_____. *Gorges and the grant of the province of Maine, 1622. A tercentenary memorial*. Printed for the State of Maine, 1923.

Cell, Gillian T. *English Activity in Newfoundland, 1577–1660*. Toronto, 1969.

Champlain, Samuel de. *Les voyages*. Paris, Jean Borjon, 1613.
_____. *Works*. Edited by H. P. Biggar. Toronto, 1922–36. Champlain Society, New Series, I–IV, and portfolio; reprinted Toronto, 1971, 7 vols.

Cushman, David. *Weymouth's Voyage*. Extracts from a paper read before a meeting of the Society in Portland, June 29, 1859. Maine Historical Society, *Collections*, vol VI, 307–18.

Davies, Robert. *The Relation of a voyage, unto New England. Began from the Lizard, the first of June 1607*. In *The historie of travaile into virginia Britannia*. Edited by R. H. Major, Hakluyt Society, First Series, no. 6, 1849.

_____. *The Relation of a voyage, unto New England. Began from the Lizard, the first of June 1607*. In B. F. DeCosta, *The Sagadahoc Colony*, Massachusetts Historical Society, *Collections*, First Series, XVIII, 1880, 82–117.

_____. *The Relation of a voyage, unto New England. Began from the Lizard, the first of June 1607*. In *New AmericanWorld: A Documentary History of North America to 1612*, 5 vols., NY, Arno Press and Hector Bye, Inc., 1979; London, MacMillan, 1979, 429–37.

_____. *The Relation of a voyage, unto New England. Began from the Lizard, the first of June 1607*. In *The English New England Voyages,1602–1608*. Edited by David B. Quinn and Alison M. Quinn, Hakluyt Society, Second Series 161, London, 1983.

Eaton, Cyrus. *Annals of Warren*. Hallowell, 1851.

_____. *History of Thomaston, Rockland, and South Thomaston*. Hallowell, ME, Masters, Smith & Co., two vols., 1865; reprinted, Courier-Gazette, Inc., 1972.

_____. *Annals of Warren*. Hallowell, 1877; reprint of 1851 edition with changes by the author, including the river explored by Waymouth.

Eckstorm, Fannie H. *The handicrafts of the modern indians of Maine*. Abbe Museum, Bulletin 3, 1932.

_____. *Indian place-names of the Penobscot Valley and the Maine coast*. Orono, Maine, University of Maine, Bulletin 44, (1941).

_____. *Old John Neptune*. Portland, ME, the Southworth-Anthoensen Press, 1945.

Gookin, Daniel. *The Historical Collections of the Indians in New England*. New York, Arno Press, 1972. Being a reprint of 1792 edition with notes added by Jeffrey H. Fiske.

Gorges, Sir Ferdinando. *A briefe relation of the discovery and plantation of New England:and of sundry accidents therein occurring, from the yeere of our Lorde M.DC.VI to this present M.DC.XXII*. In Council of New England, *Records of the Council of New England*, J. Haviland, sold by W. Bladen, 1622. Reprinted in American Antiquarian Society, *Proceedings*, 1865–67, 53–181, 24 April 1867.

_____. *A briefe narration of the original undertakings of the advancement of plantations into the parts of America. Especially showing the beginning, progress and continuence of that of New England*. In *America Painted to the Life*, by Ferdinando Gorges, the younger, [nephew of Sir Ferdinando], printed by Nathaniel Brooke, 1659.

Hakluyt, Richard. *The Principall Navigations, Voiages and Discoveries of the English nation, made by Sea or over Land, to the most remote and farthest distant Quarters of the earth at any time within the compasse of these 1500 yeeres*. Imprinted at London by George Bishop and Ralph Newberie, Deputies to Christopher Barker, Printer to the Queenes most excellent Maiestie, in the year 1589.

_____. *R. Hakluyt's Principal Navigations*. Reprinted by Hakluyt Society, 10 vols., Glasgow, James MacLehose and Sons, Publishers to the University, 1903–05.

Jenney, Charles Francis. *The fortunate island of Monhegan: A historical monograph*. Worcester, MA, American Antiquarian Society, vol. 31, 1922.

Levermore, Charles Herbert, ed. *Forerunners and Competitors of the Pilgrims and Puritans: or Narratives of Voyages made by Persons other than the Pilgrims and Puritans of the Bay Colony to the Shores of New England During the first Quarter of the Seventeenth Century, 1601–1625 with Especial Reference to the Labors of Captain John Smith in Behalf of the Settlement of New England*. Brooklyn, NY, the New England Society of Brooklyn, 1912.

Maine Historical Society. *The Collections of the Maine Historical Society*. Ten vols., with index at vol. X, Portland, ME, published for the society, 1865–91.

_____. *Tercentenary of Martin Pring's first voyage to the coast of Maine, 1603–1903*. Portland, ME, published for the Maine Historical Society by the Lefavor-Tower Co., 1903.

_____. *Waymouth Tercentenary, An Account of the Celebration of the Landing of George Waymouth on the Coast of Maine*. July 1905. No publisher listed, but certainly same as above on Pring.

_____. *Tercentenary of the landing of the Popham Colony, August 29, 1907.* Same as above.

Moody, Robert E., ed. *The Letters of Thomas Gorges, 1640–1643.* Maine Historical Society, Portland, ME, 1978.

Parks, George B. *Richard Hakluyt and the English Voyagers.* NY, Special Publication No. 10, American Geographical Society, 1928; reprinted, 1961.

Prince, George. *The voyage of Capt. Geo. Weymouth to the coast of Maine in 1605.* Maine Historical Society, *Collections,* 1857, vol. VI, 291–306.
_____. *Rosier's Narrative of Weymouth's Voyage to the Coast of Maine, in 1605, complete with remarks by George Prince, showing the River Explored to Have Been the Georges River.* Eastern Times Press, Bath, 1860.

Pring, Martin. *A voyage set out from the citie of Bristol...for the discoverie of the North part of Virginia.* In Samuel Purchas, *Hakluytus Posthumus or Purchas his Pilgrimes,* IV, 1625, 1647–57.
_____. Discussed in *Tercentenary of Martin Pring's first voyage to the Coast of Maine,1603-1903.* Papers read on November 19, 1903, before the Maine Historical Society at a meeting commemorative of the tercentenary of Martin Pring's first voyage to America,
_____. *A voyage set out from the citie of Bristol...for the discoverie of the North part of Virginia.* in H. S. Burrage, *Early English and French Voyages: Chiefly from Hakluyt, 1534–1608,* NY, Charles Scribner's Sons, 1906; reprinted NY, Barnes & Noble, Inc., 1934; reprinted NY, Barnes & Noble, Inc., 1959, 346–52.

Purchas, Samuel. *Hakluytus posthumus or Purchas his pilgrimes.* 4 vols., W. Stansby for H. Featherstone, 1625.
_____. *Hakluytus posthumus, or Purchas his pilgrimes.* Reprinted by Hakluyt Society, 20 vols., Glasgow, James MacLehose and Sons, Publishers to the University, 1905–07.

Quinn, David B. (with R. A. Skelton). *Richard Hakluyt, The principall navigations (1589).* 2 vols., Hakluyt Society, Extra Series 39, 1965.
_____. *Richard Hakluyt, editor: with facsimiles of Divers voyages (1582), and a journal of several voyages into New France (1580).* 2 vols., Amsterdam, Theatrum Orbis Terrarum, Ltd., 1967.

_____ (with Alison M. Quinn and Susan Hillier) *England and the discovery of America, 1481-1620.* NY, 1974. In *New American World: A Documentary History of North America to 1612.* 5 vols., NY, Arno Press and Hector Bye., Inc; London, MacMillan, 1979.

_____ (with Alison M. Quinn) *The English New England Voyages, 1602-1608.* Hakluyt Society, Second Series, 161, London, 1983.

Rasles, Sebastien. *A dictionary of the Abenaki language in North America.* With introduction, memoir, and notes by John Pickering. In *American Academy of Arts and Sciences,* New Series, vol. I, 1833, 375-574.

Rosier, James. *A true relation of the most prosperous voyage made in this present yeere 1605, by Captaine George Waymouth.* Eliots Court Press, George Bishop, 1605.

_____. *Extracts of a Virginian voyage made in 1605 by Captain George Waymouth.* In Samuel Purchas, *Hakluytus Posthumous or Purchas his Pilgrimes,* IV (1625), 1659-67, XVIII Hakluyt Society, 1906, 335-60.

_____. *A true relation....* Massachusetts Historical Society, *Collections,* First Series, VIII (1843), 125-57.

_____. *Rosier's narrative of Waymouth's voyage.* Edited by George Prince. Bath, ME, 1860.

_____. *Rosier's relation of Waymouth's voyage to the coast of Maine.* 1605, ed. by Henry S. Burrage. Portland, ME, 1887, Gorges Society, Publication 3.

_____. *A true relation.* In G. P. Winship, *Sailor's Narratives of Voyages Along the New England Coast (1524-1624).* (1905), 99-151.

_____. *A true relation.* H.S. Burrage, *Early English and French Voyages: Chiefly from Hakluyt, 1534-1608.* 1906, p. 353-95.

_____. *Waymouth's Voyage: Rosier.* In C. H. Levermore, *Forerunners and Competitors of the Pilgrims and Puritans.* 1912, p. 313-51.

_____. *A true relation.* In D. B. Quinn, *New American World,* III, NY, Arno Press and Hector Bye, 1979; London, Macmillan, 1979, 365-80.

_____. *Extracts of a Virginian voyage made in 1605 by Captain George Waymouth.* in D. B. Quinn, *New American World,* III, NY, Arno Press and Hector Bye, 1979; London, Macmillan, 1979, 380-91.

_____. *A true relation.* In D. B. Quinn, *The English New England Voyags 1602-1608,* Hakluyt Society, Second Series, vol. 161, 1983, 250-309.

Smith, Captain John. *A map of Virginia, with a description of the countrey*. Oxford, I. Barnes, 1612.

_____. *A description of New England*. H. Lownes for R. Clerke, 1616.

_____. *The Generall Historie of Virginia, New England & The Summer Isles, Together with The True Travels, Adventures and Observations, and A Sea Grammar*. I. D.[awson] and I. H.[aviland] for M. Sparkes, 1624.

_____. *Works*. Edited by E. Arber. Birmingham, 1884; London, 1895; edited by E. Arber and A. G. Bradley. 2 vols., Edinburgh, 1910; reprinted NY, 1967.

_____. *The Generall Historie of Virginia, New England & The Summer Isles, Together with The True Travels, Adventures and Observations, and A Sea Grammar.* 2 vols., Glasgow, James MacLehose and Sons, Publishers to the University, MCMVII.

Snow, Dean S. *Eastern Abenaki*. In *Handbook of North American Indians*. Edited by Bruce Trigger. Washington, DC, Smithsonian Institution, 1978, 137–47.

Speck, Frank G. *Penobscot Man*. Philadelphia, 1940; reprinted NY, University of Pennsylvania Press, 1970; reprinted Orono, ME, University of Maine Press, 1987.

Spencer, W. D. *Pioneers on Maine Rivers*. Portland, ME, 1930. Published by the author.

Strachey, William. *The historie of travaile into virginia Britannia*. Edited by R. H. Major, Hakluyt Society, First Series, no. 6, 1849.

_____. *The historie of travell into Virginia Britania*. Edited by Louis B. Wright and Virginia Freund, Hakluyt Society, Second Series, no. 103, 1953.

Thayer, Henry C., ed. *The Sagadahoc Colony*. Gorges Society Publication 4, Portland, ME, 1892.

Thornton, J. W. *Ancient Pemaquid*. In Maine Historical Society, *Collections*, vol. II, 1857, 155–57.

Trigger, Bruce, ed. *The Northeast*. in *Handbook of North American Indians*, XV, Washington, DC, Smithsonian Institution, 1978.

U.S. Government. *Chart No. 13009, Gulf of Maine and Georges Bank.* NOAA, National Ocean Service, March 1985.

_____. *Chart No. 13309, Penobscot River.* NOAA, National Ocean Service, 24th Edition, 1988.

_____. *Tidal Current Tables, Atlantic Coast of North America.* NOAA, National Ocean Service, 1992.

_____. *Pilot No. 169201—Pilot Chart of the North Atlantic Ocean.* Defence Mapping Agency, March 1992.

_____. *Chart No. 13006, West Quoddy Head to New York.* NOAA, National Ocean Service, March 1997.

_____. *Chart No. 13260, Bay of Fundy to Cape Cod.* NOAA, National Ocean Service, July 1999.

Waymouth, Captain George. Discussed in *Waymouth Tercentenary, An Account of the Celebration of the Landing of George Waymouth on the Coast of Maine.* Addresses made on the occasion of the tercentenary celebration at the Georges Islands and at Thomaston on July 6, 1905. No publisher, no author, no date.

Willoughby, Charles C. *The antiquities of the New England Indians.* Cambridge, MA, Harvard University, Peabody Museum, 1935.

Winship, George P., ed. *Sailors' Narratives of Voyages Along the New England Coast, 1524–1624.* Boston, 1905.

Wood, William. *New England's prospect.* Thomas Cotes for Iohn Bellamie. 1634.

_____. *New England's prospect.* ed. by C.[harles] D.[eane], Boston, 1865. Prince Society, Publication 1; reprinted NY, 1967.

Wroth, Lawrence C. *The voyages of Giovanni da Verrazano.* New Haven, Yale University Press, 1970.

Index

True Relation, A (James Rosier),
14, 15, 16, 19–93, 109–10

Union River, Maine, 111

Velasco, Alonzo de, xi
Verrazano, Giovanni, 4, 6, 7, 10
Vinalhaven, Maine, 75
Virginia Company, 14, 16, 22,
27, 108, 109
Virginia, 4, 6, 7, 9, 27, 119–20
Waldoboro, Maine, 104
Waterworks Falls, 81
Way, Thomas, 104
Waymouth, Captain George:
logs, ix; voyage of 1605,
ix–x, 5, 8, 10–15, 22–93,
107–08, 111, 115, 118,
121–25; voyage of 1602, 5;
Jewell of Artes, 5
weather, 45
wells, 41, 42
Wesserunskek. *See* Skowhegan.
whaling. *See* Native Americans.
Williams, Captain John Foster, x
Winslade, Tristram, 9–10
Witheridge, Captain, 103
Works (Samuel de Champlain),
59
Wriothesley, Henry. *See*
Southampton, Earl of.
Zouche, Sir John, 14